GENIUS
JOKES

Inspiring | Educating | Creating | Entertaining

Brimming with creative inspiration, how-to projects, and useful
information to enrich your everyday life, Quarto Knows is a favorite
destination for those pursuing their interests and passions. Visit our
site and dig deeper with our books into your area of interest:
Quarto Creates, Quarto Cooks, Quarto Homes, Quarto Lives,
Quarto Drives, Quarto Explores, Quarto Gifts, or Quarto Kids.

This edition published in 2019 by Crestline,
an imprint of The Quarto Group
142 West 36th Street, 4th Floor
New York, NY 10018 USA
T (212) 779-4972 **F** (212) 779-6058
www.QuartoKnows.com

First published in 2018 by Rock Point, an imprint of The Quarto Group,
142 West 36th Street, 4th Floor, New York, NY 10018, USA

Crestline titles are also available at discount for retail, wholesale, promotional, and bulk purchase. For
details, contact the Special Sales Manager by email at specialsales@quarto.com or by mail at The
Quarto Group, Attn: Special Sales Manager, 100 Cummings Center, Suite 265-D, Beverly, MA 01915,
USA.

10 9 8 7 6 5 4 3 2 1

ISBN: 978-0-7858-3798-5

MIX
Paper from
responsible sources
FSC www.fsc.org FSC® C008047

Editorial Director: Rage Kindelsperger
Creative Director: Merideth Harte
Managing Editor: Erin Canning
Cover and Interior Design: Ashley Prine

Printed in China

WHAT'S SO FUNNY

GENIUS JOKES

LAUGH YOUR WAY THROUGH

HISTORY • SCIENCE • CULTURE

& LEARN A LITTLE SOMETHING ALONG THE WAY

Frank Flannery

"The most exciting phrase to hear in science, the one that heralds the most discoveries, is not 'Eureka!' but 'That's funny . . .'"

—Isaac Asimov (probably . . . maybe)

CONTENTS

INTRODUCTION

AS WITH THE EPIGRAPH FOR THIS BOOK, JOKES HAVE a long, meandering, crisscrossing, indeterminate history. It's almost impossible to ever say with conviction who told a particular joke first, as jokes live and breathe—and breed—out in the world much of their own accord. Jokes themselves are probably as old as language. Maybe even older. Maybe the first good laugh happened spontaneously when one caveman farted and another one broke out in uncontrollable giggles that were such a good distraction from the perpetual hunger and fear that was the life of a caveman, they started farting on purpose to make one another laugh. It's possible! The fact is, recorded jokes are at least as old as the ancient Greeks (see page 104), but even the jokes they wrote down were acknowledged as being old gags at the time of their recording.

The impulse to make another person laugh is seemingly an innate part of human nature, right up there with eating and copulating. According to the esteemed, cigar-chomping psychiatrist Sigmund Freud, "A joke is a judgement which produces a comic contrast; it has already played a silent part in caricature, but only in judgement does it attain its peculiar form and the free sphere of its unfolding." What the incredibly dry and not-at-all-droll doctor is trying to say is that jokes are funny because they say something unexpected. They make a twist or turn that is unpredictable but has a certain sense to it, making it amusing. It's what physicist Richard Feynman would call "the kick of discovery."

This book is chock-full of just that kind of kick. While there are endless jokes out there that any old joe would get—bar jokes, light-bulb jokes, knock-knock jokes, racy jokes, gross jokes, baby jokes, fat jokes, blonde jokes, the categories go on and on—*Genius Jokes* is devoted to the kind of jokes only the learned would laugh at. Jokes that require some kind of background knowledge to get what's so funny. You need to know a bit about the uncertainty principle (page 12), counting in binary (page 32), the surrealist movement (page 39), Charles Dickens (pages 53 and 59), neural firings (page 146), sentence structure (pages 73, 76, 89, 90, and 91), the Ottoman Empire (page 109), continental philosophy (page 122), or Buddhist koans (page 154) to find the punchlines provided here funny. How superiorly erudite, right?

Wrong! *Genius Jokes* doesn't just give you the gag, it gives you the explanation about why the punchline hits. Pithy descriptions of the principles, philosophies, histories, and literature are provided with each joke, so when you retell it to your friends and family and they stare back blankly, you can look down your nose and say, "Well, my simple companion . . . ," and relate what they're missing right before they bop you one on your turned-up nose.

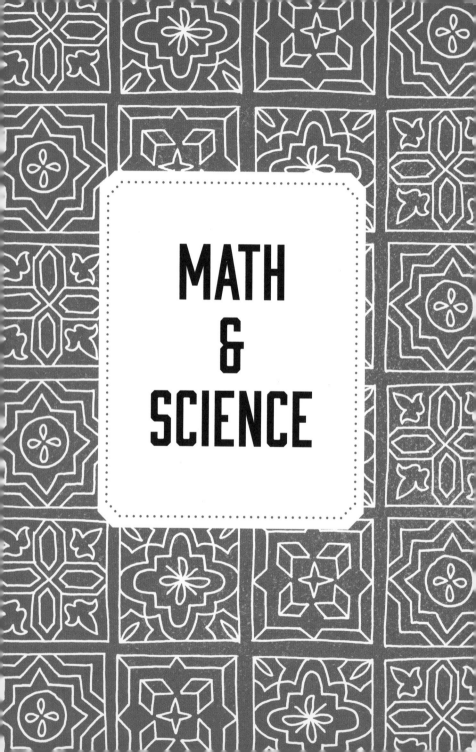

MATH
&
SCIENCE

MODERN NERDS ARE BEATING DOWN THE DUSTY old image of guys in lab coats and horn-rimmed glasses solemnly chalking out equations on the board. Scientists like Bill Nye and Neil deGrasse Tyson are out there cracking up audiences while they educate, and T-shirts that say things like "Paleontologists do it in the dirt" are on the rise, all of which adds more than a little levity to the perception of the math and science culture. While dorks, nerds, and the numerically inclined were once the punchlines of jokes (and the punching bags of bullies if we are to believe most movies from the 1980s), today they are rich celebrities, beloved sitcom characters, and potentially the saviors of all mankind as they figure out how to cure disease, feed the world, and stop global warming—and if all that fails, they'll be the ones to rocket us off the smoking heap we once called Earth. Go, smart people!

CLASSIC HEISENBERG

Heisenberg is speeding around, trying to find a hall where he's supposed to give a lecture. Just as he thinks he recognizes the street he's been looking for, a cop pulls him over and tells him, "You were going 93.287 miles an hour!"

Heisenberg exclaims, "Great! Now I'm lost!"

WHAT'S SO FUNNY?

While this joke depends on Werner Heisenberg's uncertainty principle, it's certainly a classic in the realm of science gags. The principle states that when it comes to quantum particles, the more precisely you know the speed of a particle, the *less* precisely you can know its position. So in our joke, once Heisenberg realizes how fast he was going, he no longer knows where he is. Ba dum ch!

WHAT SIDE ARE YOU ON?

If you're not part of the solution,

you're part of the precipitate.

. . . .
WHAT'S SO FUNNY?
. . . .

In chemistry, a mixture of two or more substances is called a *solution*. If a chemical reaction using a liquid solution creates a solid, that solid is called a *precipitate*. Science nerds unite in their love of this classic joke that plays on the revolutionary mantra of the '60s, "If you're not part of the solution, you're part of the problem."

THAT'S ON YOU

Schrödinger is speeding down a road in Vienna one day and gets pulled over. He keeps looking around nervously and drumming his fingers on the wheel. The cop, noticing Schrödinger's agitation, decides to search the car. When the officer opens the trunk, he yells up to Schrödinger, "Hey, do you know you have a dead cat back here?"

Schrödinger yells back, "Well I do now!"

WHAT'S SO FUNNY?

Austrian physicist Erwin Schrödinger's infamous cat is part of a thought experiment meant to highlight how the Copenhagen interpretation of quantum mechanics can be fairly nutty. It holds that on the subatomic level there is such a thing as the superposition, meaning that if the state of an object is unknown, until you measure it, it won't actually have a state, but will be in all possible states at once. The act of measuring effects, even causes, the results, but before you do the measuring, all outcomes actually exist together, superimposed on each other.

Schrödinger illustrated this by supposing (let's hope he only supposed it!) that a cat was locked in a steel box with a tiny bit of radioactive stuff that has a fifty-fifty chance of a single atom decaying over

an hour. If an atom *does* decay, then an elaborate deathtrap would spring and kill the cat. If an atom *doesn't* decay, then the kitty lives to meow another day. But since the box is closed off from observation (i.e., measurement), according to the superposition, the cat would be alive and dead at the same time.

I'M GOING TO NEED YOU TO COME WITH ME

What did the photon say to airport security when they asked if it had any luggage?

"Nope, I am traveling light!"

WHAT'S SO FUNNY?

Photons are teensy-weensy (subatomic particle teensy-weensy) packets of electromagnetic radiation of various frequencies that range from gamma rays to x-rays to visible light to infrared to radio waves. All photons travel at the speed of light in a vacuum, such as space or the no-man's-land of airport security. So, when the photon replies that it is traveling light, it literally is light that is traveling. Meaning it probably doesn't have any luggage.

BACK IN MY DAY . . .

What did the old physicist say to the
young physicist?

Entropy isn't what it used to be.

. . . .
WHAT'S SO FUNNY?
. . . .

In the most layman of senses, entropy is the degree of disorder in a system. A system is like a hot pot of soup or the universe. In thermodynamics it's the measure of unusable energy in a closed system due to the disorderly conduct of the atoms and molecules in the system. It's like if you have ten people working together, and they're all bright-eyed and bushy-tailed, they'll output ten people's worth of work. But if, say, four of them have been hitting the bottle, then you'll only get maybe five or six people's worth of work, because of the drunk and disorderly folks. The relevant part of this to our joke is that entropy is always on the move, from orderly to disorderly when things heat up or in reverse as things cool down.

BABY NEEDS A NEW PAIR OF REACTORS!

Why did the thermodynamicist have a gambling problem?

Because there's no winning, there's no breaking even, but you still can't stop playing.

. . . .
WHAT'S SO FUNNY?
. . . .

This type of interpretation of the laws of thermodynamics, also known as the "game version" of the laws of thermodynamics, may have first been thought up by the physicist C. P. Snow, the sci-fi novelist Isaac Asimov, the poet Allen Ginsberg, the lyricist Charlie Smalls for his song "You Can't Win," or someone we'll never know about. No matter who posited it first, it puts the first three laws of thermodynamics in a light most gamblers can understand. There's a closed system of energy (or money the gambler and the bet taker have). That energy (or moolah) cannot be created or destroyed. That's rule one, and that being the case, the gambler can't come out on top, because additional cash can't be created. Rule two states that entropy will increase over time, meaning things break down, so gamblers can't break even—they can only get to a more broken down spot. Third, the kicker, that as temperatures drop to absolute zero, entropy will reach a constant minimum, but it doesn't stop. It can't stop, and so gamblers can't stop playing.

66 When a man sits with a pretty girl for an hour, it seems like a minute. But let him sit on a hot stove for a minute—and it's longer than any hour. That's relativity. 99

—Albert Einstein

WHILE PERHAPS NOT THE MOST SCIENTIFIC explanation, Einstein told his secretary to describe relativity in this way to reporters and any other interested laypeople. Granted, it is a lot easier to understand than trying to imagine how mass and energy warp space-time, but it's also fairly far from accurate. What it does show is that Einstein had a bit of humor in his genius. He wrote letters filled with jokes to Johanna Fantova, his last girlfriend (or girl friend, it's not totally clear). According to one of Fantova's diary entries, Einstein received a parrot for his seventy-fifth birthday, and when he decided the bird was depressed, he told it jokes to try to cheer it up. Too bad Fantova didn't write down any of those!

YOU'RE IT!

Einstein, Newton, and Pascal are playing hide-and-seek. It's Einstein's turn to be it, so he closes his eyes and starts counting, "Eins, zwei, drei . . ." Pascal runs off and hides under a big bush. Newton runs over to a nearby driveway, takes out some chalk, and draws a box around him that is one meter long on all four sides. As soon as Einstein opens his eyes, he sees Newton and says, "What are you doing? I found you immediately, Newton!"

Newton says, "Nah-ah! I am one Newton per square meter, so I'm actually Pascal!"

WHAT'S SO FUNNY?

Oh, Sir Isaac Newton, you rascal! In this highly improbable game with physicists who weren't even alive at the same time, Newton has hidden himself as Blaise Pascal in the lowercase, unit-of-measurement sense of pascal. A pascal is used to measure pressure, and one pascal is indeed equal to one newton (again in the lowercase, unit-of-measurement sense) per square meter. One newton (a unit of force) is needed to accelerate one kilogram of mass at one meter per second in the direction in which the force is being applied. It's also a cookie.

I'LL HAVE ANOTHER

A neutrino walks through a bar . . .

WHAT'S SO FUNNY?

The setup is the punchline in this *particular* take on the classic category of bar jokes. A neutrino is a subatomic, elementary particle with the smallest amount of mass of anything around. It's mass is so small (How small was it?) that it doesn't really react with other particles and can easily pass through most matter.

A DEBUNKED JOKE

"Hey! We don't allow anything faster than light in here!" yelled the bartender.

A neutrino walks into a bar.

It was once thought that neutrinos were faster than light, but that theory has been debunked left to right, up and down. If it *was* true, though, and the neutrino was going faster than the speed of light, then it effectively would be moving backward in time because science. If it *was* true and it *was* effectively moving backward in time, then you'd get the punchline before the setup.

TRUST NO ONE

Why didn't the physicist trust atoms?

Because they make up everything!

. . . .
WHAT'S SO FUNNY?
. . . .

Atoms are in fact the building blocks of all matter. They are the smallest basic pieces and therefore can be said to make up every last bit of matter in the known universe. While they *make up* matter in the sense that they compose it, you could, if you wanted to be a funny little scientist, take it to mean they lie about everything in the universe. And who knows, maybe if your current scientific understanding of matter someday, somehow gets turned on its head, maybe we'll think atoms were made up after all. Then again, probably (make that *absolutely*) not.

THIS ONE'S ON THE HOUSE

A neutron walks into a bar and asks for a drink. Then another. Then another. At the end of the night, it asks the bartender, "OK, how much do I owe you?"

The bartender replies, "No charge!"

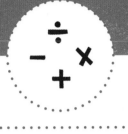

A neutron is an elementary particle that is part of an atom's nucleus. (That is, unless the atom is hydrogen, which has taken a hard pass on neutron, having only a proton in its nucleus.) It is neutral, meaning it has no charge. It might be positively sauced at the end of this joke, but it still won't get charged.

WORKING HARD FOR THE MONEY

Why is power so stressed out?

Because it has to work overtime!

Do you know how to find power? No, it's nothing to do with money or reading Tony Robbins's books. You find it by dividing work by time, or another way to say that is *work over time*. Work in this case is the force that acts on an object and causes it to move. Time being, well, time. There's probably a work force joke in there somewhere, but I can't seem to find it!

WINK WINK, NUDGE NUDGE

What did the astrophysicist tell his buddies when he returned from a weekend-long conference?

"What happens in the event horizon stays in the event horizon."

WHAT'S SO FUNNY?

The punchline (but not the setup, which was added by yours truly to give this quip a more traditional joke format) was created by Matt Crawford, an astrophysicist at Fermilab. It reached all across the country when his son, Owen, who was just twelve at the time, told and then *explained* this wisecrack to Lesley Stahl on *60 Minutes*. It works as many science jokes do, because it is literally true. The event horizon is the boundary around a black hole where the gravity becomes so great that nothing can escape it, not even light. It is the point of no return, so anything that happens there stays there. End of story.

A TRULY ENDANGERED SPECIES

Why did the bear dissolve when it
jumped in the water?

It was polar!

What's So Funny?

Wakka wakka wakka! Wait, that's the wrong kind of bear. The bear
in this joke is polar, but in the molecular sense (as opposed to the
endangered cold-weather-mammal sense). This means that one end of
a molecule has a positive charge and the other has a negative charge;
there are two poles, meaning they are dipoles. Water molecules are
themselves dipoles, meaning they too have negative and positive
charges on their ends, so when you add other equally confused
molecules into the mix, the water dipoles get in on the structures of
the other molecules, because they all have the same kind of poles.

I WANT TO PRESS CHARGES

A sodium ion rushes into a police station and exclaims, "I need to file a report."

The officer on duty says, "OK, just calm down. What's wrong?"

"I lost an electron!" the atom says.

"Are you sure?" asks the officer.

"I'm positive!" yells the atom.

. . . .
WHAT'S SO FUNNY?
. . . .

An atom has a nucleus (made of protons and neutrons) and electrons that orbit it. An ion is an atom that has lost or gained an extra electron. Electrons have a negative charge, so if it gains an electron, the ion becomes negatively charged, but if it loses an electron, as with our frantic sodium ion in this joke, its charge becomes *positive*.

BEFORE THE ATOMIC RIGHTS MOVEMENT

Helium, argon, and neon float into a bar and ask for a round of drinks.

The bartender says, "Sorry, but we don't serve your type in here."

The gases, being noble, don't react.

KEEP IT GOING

Sodium, however, who was sitting at the bar and had just taken a sip of water, absolutely *exploded*!

WHAT'S SO FUNNY?

Helium, argon, and neon are all part of a group of the periodic table known as the noble gases. They are fairly inert, meaning they don't react to things like heat and typically reaction-inducing substances like acids. In other words, they are mad chill.

Sodium, on the other hand, is a metal that is incredibly reactive. When it comes in contact with water, it reacts so violently that it might actually catch fire and essentially explode.

A PI-STAR RATING

What do you call music you buy on the black market that got 3.14159265359 out of five stars?

Pi-rated music!

What's So Funny?

This one should get a drum-hit-cymbal-crash for sure! Pi is the ratio of the diameter of a circle to its circumference, that ratio being 3.14159265359 on and on into infinity. It has been figured out into the quadrillionths so far, which is fairly amazing and well beyond the needs of this joke, which is just using the word *pi* to make fun of making illegal, unlicensed copies of media, a process known as *pirating*.

YOU GOTTA BE CLID'ING ME

Why did the chicken cross the Möbius strip?

To get to the same side.

WHAT'S SO FUNNY?

A Möbius strip is a mind-bending little piece of geometry. It's a surface that is three-dimensional yet has only one side. You get it by taking a rectangular strip, twisting it 180 degrees, and then joining the ends. If you followed the surface of a Möbius strip, you'd cover the entire shape, back and front, before getting back to your starting position. So, if a chicken were to cross one side, it would end up on the same side, confused and a bit shaken.

LITERAL LUNCH

A woman on a road trip is driving through a small town looking for some lunch. She passes a diner that has a sign boasting that it has "The Meanest Chili in the State!" As an avid chili lover, she stops and orders a bowl. When the waiter brings her the bill he asks, "So, how did you like the chili?"

The woman, who was not impressed by the meal, replies, "Just as the sign promised, it was average!"

WHAT'S SO FUNNY?

While the sign meant "meanest" to be a slangy way of saying "best" and maybe even "spiciest," the woman, who was disappointed in the chili, decided to play on that phrasing by using the mathematical definition of "mean." In that sense, the mean is the average, which is exactly what the woman thought about her lunch.

NOT THAT KIND OF MULTIPLICATION

Why did the biologist fail mathematics?

Because he thought multiplication was the same as division.

· · · · · · · · · · · · · · · · · · ·

WHAT'S SO FUNNY?

· · · · · · · · · · · · · · · · · · ·

Biologically speaking, many organisms reproduce through cell division in which the mommy and the daddy each contribute half of the genetic material that makes up the baby. The daddy's sperm and the mommy's ovum (both are types of cells known as *haploid gametes*) combine to form a zygote cell. This cell then divides and divides and divides to make a baby. So, to our improbably hapless biologist, it means the same thing for an organism to *multiply* and to *divide*. Sort of.

COMPUTERS THINK THEY'RE SO SMART

Why do computers count in binary?

Because it's as easy as OI IO II.

WHAT'S SO FUNNY?

Binary code isn't in fact easy in any immediately apparent way. But if you are highly, unceasingly logical, like a computer, it is actually very simple and even elegant. It's a two-number system of 0s and 1s in which everything is represented by combinations of those two numbers. So, while our normal counting system is a base-ten system using ten symbols ("0" through "9") and recombining those in sequence to count to infinity, binary uses just two symbols, "0" and "1," to do the same thing. So in our regular system, to get past "9" you add "1" to the front of the number and reset to one or more "0" on the end. 9 + 1 = 10. 99 + 1 = 100. In binary you have just two symbols, so you have to reset much sooner. Zero is easy, it's "00." And one is "01"—not too hard. But to get to two, you have to reset to "0" and then add "1" to the left of the number, so two is "10." Since this is a base-two system, when you add one to two (or "01" to "10" in binary) three is "11," but to go up, you have to reset again, adding a "1" to the left and resetting the rest to "0" giving you "100" as four. It's SOOOO simple.

DO YOU THINK THEY KNOW MEGADETH?

Have you heard the band Nine Hundred Ninety-Nine Megabytes?

Their album is great, but they haven't gotten any gigs yet.

What's So Funny?

If you're talking computer memory, you're talking bits and bytes. A byte has 8 bits and is the basic unit of computer memory, as you need 8 bits to make a single character such as a letter. There are 1,000,000 bytes in a megabyte, and 1,000 megabytes in a gigabyte, which is colloquially known as a *gig*. So, if the band has 999 megabytes, it doesn't have a gig. Hip computer geeks liked this joke before it was cool.

HE JUST DOESN'T GET IT

A woman sent her computer-programmer husband to the farm stand, instructing him to "buy four apples, and if they have fresh eggs, get a dozen."

The programmer asks the woman working the stand if they have fresh eggs, and she tells him that they do.

So he says, "Great! Then give me a dozen apples, please."

. . . .
WHAT'S SO FUNNY?
. . . .

In programming, you have to be absolutely precise about your instructions, because computers, like programmer husbands, will do only literally what you tell them to do. The wife's if/then request was clear in a colloquially this-is-how-normal-people-speak-and-everyone-gets-it sense, but in the world of program code, she gave him instructions on buying apples. She never says buy eggs; she just makes the apple purchase quantity dependent on the having or not having of fresh eggs. Depending on how long they've been married, she found this outcome either adorable or exasperating.

SIT. STAY. GOOD DIPOLE!

What's the difference between a dog
and a dipole?

***Every dog has it's day, but a dipole
only has a moment!***

WHAT'S SO FUNNY?

A dipole is two equal but oppositely charged electric or magnetic
poles that are a small distance apart. When one of those poles has
a stronger pull on electrons (which have a negative charge), that
side becomes a little more negatively charged then the other side,
which has a slight positive change. The distance between the separate
charges is the *dipole moment*.

ART
&
LITERATURE

EVEN IF YOU'RE NOT A MICHELANGELO WITH MARBLE or a Wordsworth with, uh, words, you can be a true jester of the fine arts. This chapter is loaded with literary laughs, packed with painting puns, and decked out with Dickensian good humor. These jokes are perfect for when you find yourself in awkward, halted conversation at an art opening, pressed into talking to an English professor at an interminable dinner party, or trapped on a lifeboat adrift in the Pacific with a sculptor and a librarian. Who among us can say we've never found ourselves in at least one of those situations? And even if you never end up ticking away the time in a stalled elevator with a mixed-media performance artist whose claim to fame involves something with knives, goats, ketchup, flowers, and an opera sung in reverse, at least you'll feel prepared for just such a scenario after reading this chapter.

IT'S ELEMENTARY! OR IS IT ELEMENTAL?

Sherlock Holmes and his faithful companion, Dr. Watson, are camping in the English countryside, staking out a case. Sherlock wakes up late at night, and then wakes up Dr. Watson as well, asking him, "Watson, what do you see when you look up?" Watson replies, "I see the millions of stars of the Milky Way."

"What do you deduce from them, my boy?" Sherlock asks.

"Well, let me see. Based on the position of Orion, I know we're in the Northern Hemisphere in summer, and it's about three o'clock in the morning. Mars is in Taurus. And, let's see, I think it will be a drizzly day. What do you see, Holmes?"

"That someone has stolen our tent!"

WHAT'S SO FUNNY?

The highly logical detective Sherlock and his well-intentioned but not-quite-as-bright companion, Watson, have maintained their popularity since the 1887 publication of *A Study in Scarlet*. In fact, the enigmatic detective is so dang popular that he's the most used cultural character of all time. Sherlock is known for his immaculate observations and

deductive reasoning, whereas Watson is known for his being there while Sherlock is brilliant. Watson does make logical leaps of his own in their adventures, but he always falls short of the glittering heights of his friend's observations, so this joke hits on the nose the nature of this famed Victorian bromance.

SALVADOR DALÍ'S FAVORITE JOKE*

How many surrealists does it take to screw in a light bulb?

Banana!

WHAT'S SO FUNNY?

Oh, the surrealists. They'd laugh at anything and nothing, the combination of which was probably doubly hilarious to them. This cultural movement, founded in the 1920s, wanted to erase the bounds between reality and dream and juxtapose irrational combinations of things like a tiger leaping from a fish's mouth only to sneeze out another tiger that was chasing a rifle (thank you, Salvador Dalí!). So, if you ask about light bulbs and get a banana instead, you've made a fairly surrealist leap yourself.

*Not really.

THIS TIPS THE SCALES

The composer was on his way to deliver a manuscript, when he called his wife and cried, "Oh no! I'm in real 𝄞! I've done something accidental—I ran over something # and now I have a ♭."

To which she said, "I'm sorry, can you 𝄇 that?"

You need to know a bit about music notation to get in on this gag:

𝄞 is a treble clef.

# indicates a sharp note.

♭ indicates a flat note.

𝄇 means repeat.

Sharps and flats are accidentals, meaning they are notes played out of the scale, or key, in which the music is written.

So, this composer— let's just assume he has unkempt hair, is fairly absentminded, and is riding a bike that's not properly fit to him—called his wife to say, "Oh no! I'm in real trouble! I've done something accidental— I ran over something sharp and now I have a flat." The wife, who is probably none too surprised to get a distressed call from her eccentric husband, asks him to repeat what sort of trouble he's in this time.

WHO SAYS WOMEN AREN'T FUNNY?

Two ladies walk into a bar and start talking to each other about **the Bechdel test**.

WHAT'S SO FUNNY!?

The Bechdel test was developed by the writer, cartoonist, and all-around awesome human Alison Bechdel as a commentary on the roles women play in movies. It first appeared in 1985 in her comic strip *Dykes to Watch Out For* in which one character says she only sees movies if they follow three simple rules: (1) There are more than two women in the cast (2) who talk to each other (3) about anything that isn't a man. Finding that none of the movies showing pass the test, the two ladies go home.

A shocking number of movies don't pass this test, which has a shockingly low bar. From critically acclaimed classics, such as *The Godfather*, *Citizen Kane*, and even *Casablanca*, to many of today's blockbusters, women just aren't getting representation commensurate with the percentage that they make up when it comes to butts in theater seats.

NO SAD SONGS ON THAT JUKEBOX

B♭, E♭, and G♭ walk into a bar and all order beers, but the bartender says, "I'm sorry, but *we don't serve minors.*"

KEEP IT GOING

To which B♭ says, "Aw, come on, we'll be out of here in no time flat. Don't make us *BEG*!"

WHAT'S SO FUNNY?

Together B♭, E♭, and G♭ make up the chord E-flat minor. And, as any reputable bartender will tell you, they don't serve minors. Perhaps it wasn't terribly couth for the B-flat to BEG for a beer, but minor chords are usually melancholy types.

DON'T GET DIZZY

M.C. Escher walks into a bar. The bartender says to him, "Hey, I want to let you in on a joke. *OK, M.C. Escher walks into a bar. The bartender says to him, 'Hey, I want to let you in on a joke. OK, M.C. Escher walks into a bar. The bartender says to him, "Hey, I want to let you in on a joke. OK, M.C. Escher walks into a bar. The bartender says to him, 'Hey, I want to let you in on a joke. OK, M.C. Escher walks into a bar . . .'"""*

WHAT'S SO FUNNY?

M.C. Escher is one of the most famous Dutch graphic artists of the twentieth century, especially in the most-stared-at-art-on-dorm-room-walls-probably-by-stoners category. He is known for his infinitely reflective, symmetrical patterns, in which swans or lizards fit together in repetition, just like this joke! What this joke lacks in iconic, enduring, genre-creating originality, it makes up for in length.

I WOULDN'T WANT TO MEET
HIM ON THE BEACH

Why did Franz Kafka cross the road?

He had received an official letter from an unknown bureaucratic agency informing him he was to appear before the court because his chickens had violated an as-yet-undisclosed ordinance, and while Kafka was unsure of when his trial would be, he had the address of the courthouse, and so would wait there for however long it took.

BONUS JOKE

Why did Franz Kafka cross the road?

He has no idea. He just woke up covered in feathers with a compulsion to cross the road.

WHAT'S SO FUNNY?

Famed Eastern European novelist Franz Kafka is remembered for his surreal, existential work. His novel *The Trial* tells the tale of an average joe, named K., who gets arrested and tried by an unknown agency for unknown crimes, and (metaphorically) drowns in the red tape of a looming yet unreachable bureaucracy (metaphorically speaking. Spoiler alert: He actually dies when a couple of warders stab him in the heart. Funny stuff!). That's the first disturbing reason for Kafka crossing the road. The bonus joke relates to perhaps his most famous work, his short story *The Metamorphosis*, in which another average joe wakes up one morning inexplicably transformed into an enormous cockroach-y insect with cockroach-y desires. And if there's one thing we know about chickens, it's that their fondest desire is to cross the road.

THIS ONE'S FOR THE BABY BOOMERS

Aristotle Onassis was looking to buy a house in Hollywood. His Realtor took him to see a bunch of mansions, including one that once belonged to Buster Keaton of silent-film fame. The paparazzi snapped a photo of Onassis and sold it to a newspaper, which printed it in the Real Estate section with the caption ***"Aristotle contemplating the home of Buster."***

WHAT'S SO FUNNY?

OK, you might have to be receiving Social Security to be old enough to get this one, but the punchline really made the rounds in the early '60s. Back then, Rembrandt's painting *Aristotle Contemplating the Bust of Homer* had just sold to the Metropolitan Museum of Art in New York for $2.3 million, the most money ever paid for a painting. EVERYONE was talking about it. Meanwhile, Aristotle Onassis was busy being famous as one of the wealthiest men in the world (he would later marry Jacqueline Kennedy, giving her the O in her epithet Jackie O. I digress.). Both Onassis and the painting being the talks about town, *Tonight Show* writer Hugh Downs imagined a scenario in which Onassis was considering the purchase of Buster Keaton's home, so he could caption a similarly imaginary photo "Aristotle

contemplating the home of Buster." People went bananas for the joke, and it went around the world in the old-timey version of viral—which was mostly just word of mouth.

AN EPIC MASH-UP

What do you get when you cross short stories by Neil Gaiman and A. A. Milne?

A Tigger warning!

WHAT'S SO FUNNY?

You may or may not recognize the name A. A. Milne, but you know his work. He's the creator of that lovable ol' bear stuffed with puff, Winnie-the-Pooh, along with Pooh's cohorts, Piglet, Eeyore, and, of course, Tigger! Oh the adorable adventures they've had! On the other hand, Neil Gaiman's name is a bit more household these days. This prolific writer has penned over a dozen novels, loads of comics, and no small amount of children's books, not to mention all those short stories, including a collection called *Trigger Warning: Short Fictions and Disturbances.*

I'M SENSING A THEME

What do you call a French story about a deformed man who tries to win the heart of a beautiful maiden who's way out of his league?

The Phantom of the Opera! Wait, no, Beauty and the Beast! Wait, no, Cyrano de Bergerac! Wait, no, The Hunchback of Notre Dame!

WHAT'S SO FUNNY?

Jeez, what's up with the French? Their eighteenth- and nineteenth-century writers really had some body issues. In each of these punch-line'd classics (a novel, a fairy tale, a play, and another novel, respectively), a man of varying deformation (skull face, beast face, schnoz face, and hunched face, I mean back) falls in love with a dazzlingly beautiful lady. Knowing he is too ugly to be loved, he tries to woo the woman through song, gifts, poetry, and heroics. Three out of four times, this doesn't really work out. The beast is the only one able to actually woo the lady and then live long enough to enjoy it.

THIS IS NOT A JOKE ABOUT A BLONDE DUMBO

What do you call it when an elephant goes to a rock concert?

Horton hears The Who!

WHAT'S SO FUNNY?

This mashup joke puts Dr. Seuss's heroic elephant at a concert of the classic British rock band The Who. While your literary and musical knowledge perhaps doesn't have to go deep to get this one, the fun of imagining this one is pretty smart. And hey, even a fictional, cartoon elephant sometimes just needs to kick back with some tunes. Though I hope it brought earplugs for the tiny Whos.

IT'S DEFINITELY NOT RUDOLPH

Which reindeer was Emily Dickinson's favorite?

Dasher!

What's So Funny?

Emily Dickinson, one of the most famous American poets of all time, defies strict categorization into a single genre. She used many poetic forms—stanzas, various meters, ABCB rhyme schemes, not ABCB rhyme schemes—and tackled just as many themes and motifs. She did, however, have one habit that makes her poems recognizable almost at a glance - the use of the dash. She used dashes for pauses, to interrupt the meter, in place of other punctuation, to connect lines, to separate lines, to maintain mystery, and for whatever else she damn well pleased. Her affinity for them was so great that, in the 1,775 poems published in the complete collection of her poetry, more than 10,000 dashes appear!

BONUS JOKE

Why didn't Emily Dickinson make it across the road?

Because she could not stop for death.

One of Dickinson's most famous poems is "Because I could not stop for Death."

MY FIVE-YEAR-OLD COULD HAVE WRITTEN THAT JOKE

How did Jackson Pollock do in art school?

He passed with flying colors.

WHAT'S SO FUNNY?

Jackson Pollock was an abstract expressionist painter who became mega famous in 1949 and has pretty much stayed famous since. He's best known for his "drip paintings," which are exactly what they sound like. He would literally let the paint fly all over the canvas, dripping it, pouring it, and flinging it every which way, because, as he himself said, "I don't paint nature, I am nature."

QUOTH THE RAVEN, "HARDY HAR HAR"

Why did the [lyrical] raven cross the road?

To rap at my chamber door.

What's So Funny?

The raven in question comes from Edgar Allan Poe's enduringly creepy and well-known poem "The Raven," in which a man lamenting the loss of his love, Lenore, is visited by the poem's eponymous black bird. In the first stanza, the raven comes "gently rapping, rapping at my chamber door." The use of "lyrical" is optional, if you want to make a play on the kind of rapping the bird enjoys engaging in.

The raven eventually finds its way into the chamber, and when the man asks its name, which I guess is what you do when birds strut into your house, the bird answers, "Nevermore." In fact, that's the only thing the bird can say. And even though the man realizes this, he continues to ask questions that cause him pain when answered with "Nevermore." He thereby drives himself bonkers via this fowl inquisition.

HOW ABOUT AN EBENEZER SCREWDRIVER?

What did the bartender say when Charles Dickens ordered a martini?

Olive or twist?

KEEP IT GOING

Dickens had **Hard Times** deciding, and he didn't have **Great Expectations** for the bartender's skills, and in the end he couldn't **Pickwick** one he wanted, and just had beer instead.

WHAT'S SO FUNNY?

Classic! Classic literature, classic joke, classic author, just classic. This punchline is a play on the title of renowned British novelist Charles Dickens's work *Oliver Twist*, which is about an adorable orphan with a heart of gold who is abused by the world until everyone gets what they deserve. Classic! You can take this joke further by referencing some of Dickens's other works: *Hard Times,* a satire about the difficulties of living in industrialized England; *Great Expectations*, which features another orphan with a heart of gold; and *The Posthumous Papers of the Pickwick Club,* a serial of loosely related adventures.

A Joke by
Leonardo da Vinci

FRANCISCAN BEGGING FRIARS ARE WONT, AT CERTAIN times, to keep fasts, when they do not eat meat in their convents. But on journeys, as they live on charity, they have license to eat whatever is set before them. Now a couple of these friars on their travels stopped at an inn, in company with a certain merchant, and sat down with him at the same table, where, from the poverty of the inn, nothing was served to them but a small roast chicken. The merchant, seeing this to be but little even for himself, turned to the friars and said: "If my memory serves me, you do not eat any kind of flesh in your convents at this season." At these words the friars were compelled by their rule to admit, without cavil, that this was the truth; so the merchant had his wish, and ate the chicken and the friars did the best they could. After dinner the messmates departed, all three together, and after traveling some distance they came to a river of some width and depth. All three being on foot—the friars by reason of their poverty, and the other from avarice—it was necessary by the custom of company that one of the friars, being barefoot, should carry the merchant on his shoulders: so having given his wooden shoes into his keeping, he took up his man. But it so happened that when the friar had got to the middle of the river, he again remembered a rule of his order, and stopping short, he looked up, like Saint Christopher, to the burden on his back and said:

"Tell me, have you any money about you?"—"You know I have," answered the other, "How do you suppose that a merchant like me should go about otherwise?" "Alack!" cried the friar. "Our rules forbid us to carry any money on our persons," and forthwith he dropped him into the water.

Da Vinci wrote down several jokes in his notebooks, this being the best one. Ah, the Renaissance. It was a period of cultural and scientific advancement, but perhaps the humor of the age lagged a bit behind.

STAY WITH ME HERE

A novice arrived at a monastery and was assigned to helping the monk who tended the gardens. The elder monk had a shock of red hair, so everyone called him Rusty, but as the novice soon learned, despite his nickname, Rusty was a very serious and strict man save for his profane outbursts, which were always directed at the plants.

The novice found these angry eruptions at the vegetation by the otherwise solemn monk to be the only bit of fun in his day, so he started writing them down. Soon his notebook was circulating around the abbey, as many of the monks got a kick out of watching Rusty yell at the vegetables. It eventually wound up with the abbot, however, who was angry at such foolishness. He called the young monk into the library, threw the notebook down on a desk, and said, "What do you call this!"

And the novice, shaking, said, "The Botanic Curses of Solemn Rusty!"

What's So Funny?

In 1988, the esteemed writer Salman Rushdie published his fourth book, *The Satanic Verses*. It was partially based on the life of the Islamic prophet Muhammad and received a fair amount of criticism from parts of the Muslim community. And by criticism, I mean death threats, most notably by Ayatollah Ruhollah Khomeini, then Supreme Leader of Iran. This joke is a lighthearted play on the words of the title and a testament to how time heals most things.

TAKE THAT, HORN SECTION!

What is the difference between a horn player and a conductor?

Usually, two measures.

What's So Funny?

BURN! Take that, horn section! This joke is at the expense of horn players, who are infamous for coming in late in orchestral performances. While it's easy to cast blame on them for coming in a measure or two late, it's not easy counting the ridiculous number of measures of rest needed before they are supposed to come blaring in flawlessly.

EITHER WAY, SHIELD YOURSELF!

What's the difference between the Arthurian Round Table and the Algonquin Round Table?

With the first, you can expect someone to die in a joust, while the others can slay while merely in jest.

ALTERNATE ENDING

One is a gang of highly skilled, brutal killers while the other is just a medieval legend.

WHAT'S SO FUNNY?

King Arthur's Round Table was populated with knights who quested for glory, saved distressed damsels, and battled dragons. They were largely men of valor and honor, though their deeds did often involve lots of violence, beheadings, and some unvirtuous behavior (Lancelot, I'm looking at you and Guinevere here). The Algonquin Round Table, on the other hand, was a lunch club in the Roaring Twenties where creative types such as Dorothy Parker, Robert Benchley, and Brock Pemberton hung out. The barbed wit of an insult from a member of this round table was as deadly as any lance. Most memorable perhaps is when a debutante said "Age before beauty" to Ms. Parker as they

were both entering a room. To which the writer rejoined, "And pearls before swine."

I'M NOT DICKENS AROUND

What did Charles Dickens say when, on his way home from vacation, his ship sunk?

It was the best of times, it was the worst of times.

THE BLUE VERSION

What did Charles Dickens say when he caught VD?

It was the best of times, it was the worst of times.

WHAT'S SO FUNNY?

The punchline is the first line of Dickens's *A Tale of Two Cities*. Arguably one of the most famous lines in literature, it succinctly illuminates the contrasts between Paris, going through the French Revolution, and London. In this context, however, it is transformed from brilliant and enduring social commentary to a joke about how things were good, and now they're bad.

IT CAN ALSO READ LIPS

What do you call a puzzlingly psychotic spaceship with six equal, square sides?

A Kubrick's cube.

. . . .
WHAT'S SO FUNNY?
. . . .

Among the many acclaimed, classic movies directed by Stanley Kubrick shines *2001: A Space Odyssey*. Part of the millennium-traversing story arc of this sci-fi masterpiece is about HAL 9000, the sentient onboard computer of the *Discovery One* spacecraft. After a malfunction, the crew decides to disable HAL, which makes HAL, well, psychotically murderous. Though Arthur C. Clarke is HAL's true creator, he and Kubrick wrote the screenplay for *2001* together, and since Clarke doesn't rhyme with the beloved six-sided puzzle the Rubik's cube, the punchline goes to Kubrick.

Shakespeare Was Hilarious!

THE PLAYS OF WILLIAM SHAKESPEARE ARE VIEWED TODAY by many to be stuffy, indecipherable elitisms enjoyed only by snooty intellectuals who think impenetrability is the soul of wit. Well, it's just not true. In his time, Shakespeare's plays were attended by all classes of folks. Walt Whitman argued that Shakespeare was "entirely fit for feudalism," meaning that he was writing for all the people in the feudalist class system, high and low. And while the language may be a bit hard to understand today, it would have all been quite natural to Elizabethan ears. Anything that seems cryptic today only seems so because our manner of speaking has changed so much. Some of that change, though, was spurred by Shakespeare himself, who was a master of the double entendre, insulted people's mamas, and introduced some rather bawdy phrases to the English language—phrases we use to this day.

The Taming of the Shrew Act II, Scene I

Petruchio: Come, come, you wasp. I' faith, you are too angry.

Katherine: If I be waspish, best beware my sting.

Petruchio: My remedy is then to pluck it out.

Katherine: Ay, if the fool could find it where it lies.

Petruchio: Who knows not where a wasp does wear his sting?
    In his tail.

Katherine: In his tongue.

Petruchio: Whose tongue?

Katherine: Yours, if you talk of tales; and so farewell.

Petruchio: What, with my tongue in your tail?

This witty little back-and-forth mixes all sorts of metaphors, but in a good way. It turns expressions of the day back and forth so that Petruchio can insult Katherine and then she him through twisting the meaning of each other's phrases. Petruchio equates Katherine, in all her nastiness, to a wasp and threatens to take out her stinger, her meanness. She accuses him of being too dumb to find it, to which he replies that it's in her butt—maybe an old English version of having a stick up one's butt. She replies it's in the tongue, in language. Whose tongue are we even talking about now? She turns it so that Petruchio is meany pants if he's making up tall tales about butts, and she bids him farewell. But he doesn't think he should leave while his tongue is in her butt, which is exactly what it sounds like.

Titus Andronicus
Act 4, Scene 2

Chiron: Thou hast undone our mother.

Aaron: Villain, I have done thy mother.

Both these guys are evil, despicable, awful, foul characters. They scheme, they murder, they rape, they are the worst. Chiron is also stupid, while Aaron is an evil genius. In this scene, Chiron is upset because his mom just had a baby, which turned out to be

Aaron's baby. (Aaron being the only Moorish guy around and the baby having a Moorish skin tone.) He accuses Aaron of ruining his mother's reputation, while Aaron replies that he has indeed done her, in the carnal sense.

Much Ado About Nothing
Act 5, Scene 2

Benedick: I will live in thy heart, die in thy lap, and be buried in thy eyes.

"To die," to an Elizabethan hip to street slang, was a euphemism for an orgasm. (The French likely got their beloved, orgasmic phrase *la petite mort* ["the little death"] from this usage.) Even the title *Much Ado About Nothing* was naughty if you knew what the kids were saying in those days, because "nothing" was used to refer to a lady's, um, lap.

Othello
Act II, Scene I

Iago: I am one, sir, that comes to tell you your daughter and the Moor are now making the beast with two backs.

Iago means "beast with two backs" in exactly the same way we mean it today: getting it on, doing it, knocking boots, i.e., sexual intercourse. While today it is considered somewhat juvenile, it is in fact Shakespearean, and Shakespeare was more juvenile than a lot of people think.

TOO DEEP, OR NOT TOO DEEP?

How many Brutuses does it take to screw in
a light bulb?

Eh, two Brute should do it.

ONE MORE

How many King Lears does it take to screw in
a light bulb?

*Just one, but he goes through two bad bulbs before
he finds one that actually works.*

· · · · · · · · · · · · · · · · · ·
WHAT'S SO FUNNY?
· · · · · · · · · · · · · · · · · ·

Though he's taken quite seriously these days, Shakespeare was actually a really funny guy! Who knows? Maybe he would have even liked
these light-bulb jokes. The first plays with a famous line from his play
Julius Caesar. As the eponymous character dies on the senate floor,
having just been stabbed by a whole gang of conspirators, including
his friend Marcus Brutus, he utters "Et tu, Brute?" which is Latin for
"And you, Brutus?"

King Lear's first two broken light bulbs refer to his two daughters who use and abuse him in his eponymous play. He says he will give the largest part of his kingdom to the one who loves him most, and his first two rat-fink daughters flatter him with saccharine effusiveness. Then the third daughter, Cordelia, the only good one, is honest with him that she cannot verbally express her love of him. The king misinterprets this depth of love for no love, and hands the kingdom over to the rats. Tragedy ensues but in the end Lear realizes Cordelia was his only non-rat offspring. Are we laughing yet?

I HEAR THAT MOBY IS A REAL . . .

Why couldn't the sea captain stop hunting whales?

It was A HABit!

. . . .
WHAT'S SO FUNNY!?
. . . .

Moby-Dick is the story of a sea captain obsessed with hunting the book's eponymous white whale. His obsession would lead to (spoiler alert!) the sinking of his ship and the deaths of himself and his entire crew, save for one man. The obsessive captain's name? Ahab.

GRAMMAR
&
LANGUAGE

JOKES ARE, IN LARGE PART, LANGUAGE AND GRAMMAR
dependent. They hinge on turns of phrase, sentence structure,
word meaning, and the finer points of speech. (Except for slap-
stick. That depends on getting your foot stuck in a bucket or
stepping on a rake and having the handle pop you in the kisser.
Also good.) Since jokes are so essentially contingent on word
choices and organization, jokes that are themselves about
grammar and language are, like, totally meta. Without things
like homonyms and sentence structure, you couldn't turn a
phrase in a surprising and funny way, so making jokes out of
those very same things is a special sort of layered joking that
true nerds will truly appreciate.

EVEN PUNCTUATION NEEDS SOME SPACE

Why did the comma dump the apostrophe?

It was way too possessive!

If you think back hard enough to elementary school grammar, you'll get this. Then again, perhaps there are enough signs out there that say things like "Mikes Bike Shop" and "Delilahs Den" to disprove that assumption.

Let us go back to basics. If you want to make a word possessive—i.e., the owner of something else—you add an apostrophe, usually followed by an *s*. So really, if the bike shop belongs to Mike, then the sign should say "Mike's Bike Shop." You might then think that the other sign should read "Delilah's Den," but in fact the den is owned by no less than seven women named Delilah, so it should read "Delilahs' Den."

GOOD THING THEY DIDN'T GO "SNAP!"

A man goes to the doctor, complaining that he keeps hearing his joints go "crack!" and "pop!" The doctor examines him, shakes her head, and says, "I am sorry to have to say this, but you've got onomatopoeia."

Alarmed, the patient says, "Oh my goodness! I've never heard of that before. What is it?"

And the doctor replies, "Well, sir, it's precisely what it sounds like."

WHAT'S SO FUNNY?

An onomatopoeia is a word that mimics the natural sound it's naming, such as *boom*, *hiss*, *crack*, and *pop*. In this joke, you could say the patient was really listening to his body!

DELIVERY ROOM EYE ROLL

A logician was in the delivery room when his
wife had their baby. The doctor immediately handed
the baby to the logician, and the wife asked, "Is it
a boy or a girl?" To which the logician, beaming,
replied, ***"Yes!"***

WHAT'S SO FUNNY?

Logic is a science, believe it or not. It studies and systemizes the
principles and criteria for making a valid argument. For something to
be a valid logical argument, in the formal sense, the conclusion must be
strictly inferred via the steps leading from the premise to the conclusion.
Suffice it to say it's a persnickety science with lots of touchy nuances
and meticulous rules around word usage and punctuation. In our little
joke, the poor, belabored wife is asking a simple enough question, but
her phrasing is ambiguous, leaving it open to be interpreted as basically
"Does the baby have a gender?" instead of what she clearly meant, "Is
it a boy, or is it a girl?" And her super-literal husband, who is probably a
real joy to be around, answers the former question.

THE PUPIL HAS BECOME THE MASTER

A professor of linguistics is teaching a 101-level course. In one of his early lectures, he tells the students, "A double negative in English forms a positive. 'You don't know nothing,' actually means the speaker thinks you know something. In some languages, though, such as Russian, Spanish, Persian, and others, a double negative is still a negative. Yet, nowhere in the world is there a language in which a double positive forms a negative."

The professor smiles, as he's quite fond of this little factoid, when a student pipes up from the back of the room, ***"Yeah, right!"***

WHAT'S SO FUNNY?

Sticking it to the Man is almost always funny. In this case, the Man is a professor who is a little too proud of his quip, which is cut down by a student who probably doesn't even realize what she or he has said. Technically speaking, "yeah" and "right" are positives, but when combined with the right sarcastic intonation, they do indeed become a negative.

"This is the type of arrant pedantry up with which I shall not put."

—Winston Churchill

YOU'VE PROBABLY HAD A GRAMMAR TEACHER WHO WAS SO doggedly devoted to the rules of grammar, they would abide them no matter how awkward or unnatural. (Said teacher would want me to use "he or she" instead of "they," but it's not my fault English comes up short in the pronoun department!)

This Winston Churchill quote refers to the odious "rule" that says you cannot end a sentence with a preposition. Someone tried to edit out a "mistake" of this variety from one of Churchill's speeches, and the quote above was his reply to their fussiness.

I say "rule" and "mistake" because it's more a misguided superstition than anything else. In the seventeenth and eighteenth centuries, some persnickety writers tried to make English grammar more like Latin. The Latin that the word *preposition* is derived from literally means "before" and "to place" (which itself is backward phrasing in English, but let's move on), so those exacting writers argued that a preposition could not go at the end of a sentence when the word itself means "to place before something." But English isn't Latin, and trying to cram English grammar into this Latin mold just gives us misshapen sentences that prick the ears and ruffle common sense. Today's grammarians and style guides all agree that you can end on a preposition if you want to.

NO ARGUMENT HERE

Only nerds know what a contrapositive is.
***And since I don't know what a contrapositive is,
then I must not be a nerd!***

WHAT'S SO FUNNY?

Nice try, but I would argue if you know enough to use the word *contrapositive* you're probably at least a bit nerdy. A contrapositive, if you're not a nerd and don't know, is a conclusion that is drawn by negating the hypothesis and the conclusion of a theorem. For example, the contrapositive of "If Jill calls then she likes me" is "If Jill *does not* call then she *does not* like me." So sad. In this gag, the speaker uses a contrapositive to prove he's not a nerd who knows what a contrapositive is. What a joker!

FAKE NEWS

Why did the reporter decide to leave "the," "a," and "an" out of his reporting?

Because everyone keeps saying articles these days are so misleading!

. . . .
WHAT'S SO FUNNY?
. . . .

Funny, or depressing? Hard to tell. The hapless reporter in this joke has misunderstood what people mean when they say "articles," mistaking them to mean the parts of speech instead of pieces of reporting. Journalism has certainly come under fire in the twenty-first century for being biased, partisan, and even fake, causing everyone to live in their own echo chamber of preferred facts. It can be said, then, that articles are indeed misleading.

I WOULDN'T GO BACK THERE

Knock knock.

Who's there?

To.

To who?

Don't you mean "To whom?"!

. . . .
WHAT'S SO FUNNY?
. . . .

Yikes. I bet you won't be visiting that house again, as a stuck-up nerd with mad grammar skills but no social graces lives there. Alas, this nerd is technically correct. *Who* is the pronoun you use as the subject of a sentence. *Who* is knocking on my door? The *who* is the subject performing the verb. Meanwhile, *whom* is used as the object of the verb or preposition in the sentence (the person the action preposition is being performed on). *Whom* do you think was knocking? To *whom* do I owe thanks for such an artful door knock?

STILL SCARY THOUGH

What do you call two crows?

An attempted murder!

There are few things creepier in the English language than calling a flock of crows a *MURDER*! Collective nouns that pertain to certain animals are called *terms of venery* (this just gets better and better!), and in addition to calling a flock of crows a murder, there are other gems in this category: a mob of kangaroos, an army of ants, a boil of hawks. Some say a group of feral cats is called a *destruction*, but it's hard to find legit etymology to that effect.

NO ONE KNOWS YOU LIKE A BROTHER DOES

Sir Mix-a-Lot likes big butts and cannot lie. His twin brother does not like big butts and cannot tell the truth. Sir Mix-a-Lot is standing in front of a door that goes to a party. His brother's in front of one that goes to a dentist's waiting room. You may ask one question to find out which door leads to the big-booty party.

This joke/riddle was adapted from musician Ranjit Bhatnagar's joke, which is a play on an age-old riddle, which was made famous in the '80s by the movie *Labyrinth*, which was made famous by David Bowie's bulge. If you can solve the riddle, then you can probably also follow that history. Give up? OK, here's the riddle-busting question:

Ask either one, "Which door would your brother say leads to big butts?"

This works because if it's Sir Mix-a-Lot himself that you're talking to, what an honor, then he *would* say his brother's door, cuz he's honest and that's what his brother the liar would say. If it's the lying brother with bad taste you're talking to, then he'll say his own door because his brother wouldn't say that and he is a liar. Either way, go through the opposite door either brother answers. Obtuse? Yes. Worth it to talk to Sir Mix-a-Lot? Also yes.

IF WILL AND HAVE SHOWED UP, IT WOULD HAVE BEEN PERFECT

Past, present, and future walked into a bar.

It was tense.

. . . .
WHAT'S SO FUNNY?
. . . .

This is perhaps *the* classic grammar joke. It plays on the three verb tenses of the English language: past, present, and future. There are a whole mess of variations on these three, but the *simple* truth is that this joke is *perfect* without them, and going on and on about them would be a *continuous* drag. (Look it up!)

THIRD TIME'S A CHARM

Three logicians go to the campus bar one night after grading papers. They walk in, and the bartender asks them, "Do all of you want a drink?"

The three look at one another, and the first logician goes, "Huh, I don't know."

The second one goes, "I don't know either."

The third one smiles triumphantly and replies, "Yes!"

. . . .
WHAT'S SO FUNNY?
. . . .

This is about as funny as semantical jokes about logicians get. Technically speaking, which is about all logicians do, the first guy can only know that he wants a drink (presuming they didn't discuss drinking before they went to the bar, but only decided on their desire to go to the place). So he can't say if they all want a drink, but if he didn't want a drink, he would have said no. The second one also only knows she wants a drink and the guy before her wants a drink, so she still can't answer in the affirmative (but similarly would have said no if she didn't want a drink). The third logician finally has all the answers he needs to say yes with confidence.

FOR VINTNER'S EYES ONLY

What makes Oloroso a perfect wine?

It's flor-less!

·····················
WHAT'S SO FUNNY?
·····················

Wine snobs love this joke! Apparently.

The things you need to know to chuckle along with vintage geeks are: Oloroso is a Spanish sherry. Flor is a film of yeast that develops on the surface of the wine during the process of making certain sherries that traditionally come from Spain and Portugal (*flor* translates to "flower" from those countries' languages). Normally a yeast film is to be avoided, and it does look rather gross, but it's needed to give sherries a fresh "bready" taste, if that's what the vintner is after. Oloroso, though, is "flor-less" (a wordplay on *flawless* if you didn't get there yet) because it is fortified early on, and the high alcohol volume kills off any flor yeast present and prevents it from coming back.

IT TAKES TWO

I came up with a single entendre, but
nobody laughed.

Then I put two together, if you catch my drift.

WHAT'S SO FUNNY?

Who's ever heard of a single entendre? Nobody! Because it doesn't exist, except in this joke, which references the *well-loved*—if you know what I mean—double entendre. A double entendre is a word or phrase that can be interpreted *multiple ways*—wink wink, nudge nudge—with one of those ways usually being a bit bawdy. The "entendre" part is from the French *entendre*, meaning "to understand," so this pidgin phrase essentially means "two understandings."

BONUS JOKE

A woman asked me for a double entendre,
so I gave it to her!

NOT THE TIME, NOAH

Did you hear the one about the dictionary maker, Noah Webster? His wife happened to find him kissing the cook, and she exclaimed, "Why Noah! I'm surprised!" To which he said, ***"My dear, I am surprised—you are astonished."***

· · · · · · · · · · · · · · · · · · ·
WHAT'S SO FUNNY?
· · · · · · · · · · · · · · · · · · ·

What a jerk! Though technically, one could argue his syntax is superior, if not terribly finicky and insensitive. He was surprised in the sense that to surprise someone is to catch them doing something. Or as Webster's 1830 dictionary defined it, "To come or fall upon suddenly and unexpectedly; to take unawares." In that way, *she* surprised *him*. And she was astonished in the ordinary ol' sense of astonished, defined in 1830 as "to stun or strike dumb with sudden fear, terror, surprise, or wonder; to amaze; to confound with some sudden passion." That last bit striking a bit too close to home perhaps for Mrs. Webster.

66 A language
is a dialect
with an army
and a navy. **99**

—Max Weinreich

THE TWENTIETH-CENTURY LINGUIST MAX WEINREICH SPECIALIZED in Yiddish, and that's the language this quote first appeared in. Weinreich credited a young man at one of his lectures with coming up with this phrase, and Weinreich wanted to make it famous. So he did!

It puts a fine and funny point on how the difference between giving something the stature of a language—putting it up there with the greats of Latin, French, Spanish, etc.—and undercutting it as a dialect—Cockney, Caribbean, and Cantonese—is largely an arbitrary distinction. You think there are going to be some strict linguistic rules governing what it means to be one or the other, but not so. Swedish and Danish, which are really, really similar, are considered languages, while Cantonese and Mandarin are considered dialects of Chinese, even though they are far less similar than the previous pair. Even Czechs and Slovaks think they are speaking different languages, though Czechoslovakia was one country until 1993!

That brings us back to the idea that a language becomes a language when its speakers have an army and a navy, meaning power and borders and such. It has nothing to do with speech itself; it's just a status thing.

A FISH JOKE FOR THE HALIBUT

A guy was on a trip to Boston and wanted to get his favorite kind of seafood for dinner. He went to the front desk and asked the concierge, "Is there any place around here where I can get scrod?"

The concierge looked up and replied, "You know, I've gotten that question countless times, but this is the first time I've heard it in the form of a passive past participle!"

WHAT'S SO FUNNY?

First you need to know that *passive* here means that the subject (the guy on the trip) of the verb (scrod) is being acted upon, or affected by the action of the verb. To the concierge, he's looking to be scrod by the end of the night. Then you need to know that a participle is a word that is formed from a verb (an action) but is acting as an adjective (a description), which here is "get scrod" as scrod will describe what the guy is once he gets his. Then a past participle is the form of a verb that indicates the action of the verb has already been performed. It also helps to know that scrod is a fish people eat for some reason.

All that said, the kicker in this joke is that there's so much grammar going on, but "scrod" is not actually any form of the verb "screw."

You can call it any pluperfect subjunctive participle shenanigan you want, and "scrod" will never actually mean "screwed." Unless you have a Boston accent, of course.

A ROSE-COLORED REARVIEW MIRROR

How is life like grammar?

The present is tense, but the past had been perfect.

WHAT'S SO FUNNY?

This little ditty on nostalgia uses wordplay on grammatical tenses. The present tense is a verb tense used to describe something that is currently or habitually happening. "The present is tense" is in fact in the present tense. Past perfect is a verb tense used to talk about something that happened before now or before some particular event. It is formed by using "had" plus a past participle—"I *had heard* this joke before grammar jokes were cool." So the punchline "the past had been perfect" uses the past perfect tense. So many layers! Well, two layers at least. *Maybe* three.

I BET HE'S REALLY SORRY NOW!

It's Christmas Eve 1843, and Ebenezer Scrooge is tired. He hadn't gotten a lot of sleep over the past couple of nights, and he fears this night will be no different. At midnight the clock gongs, ringing in Christmas Day, and when the twelfth dong sounds, an apparition appears before him saying, "I am the ghost of Christmas future perfect continuous." A little confused, Ebenezer cries, "Oh, spirit, what foul thing are you going to tell me?"

"Unless you change, you will have been wishing you'd done things differently until you're dead."

WHAT'S SO FUNNY?

This haunting joke rises from Charles Dickens' *A Christmas Carol*, which is about mean, old Ebenezer Scrooge, who is visited on Christmas Eve by spirits who convince him not to be such a jerk. "Huh?" was likely Ebenezer's reply to this garbly ghost who speaks in the future perfect continuous tense, meaning he is describing an ongoing action that will finish at some time in the future. The "ongoing action" is how Ebenezer is regretting his evil, miserly ways, and the "some time in the future" is the day Ebenezer dies.

A PURRRRFECT JOKE

What is the difference between a kitty cat
and a comma?

*The first is independent and has its claws before
the paws, while the other has a pause before its
independent clause!*

. . . .
WHAT'S SO FUNNY?
. . . .

This wordplay is perfect for everyone's favorite bookish cat lady—and we all have one of those in our lives.

A cat's claws are before, in the sense of *in front of*, its paws when the cat is in attack mode and its claws are out, and we've all seen cats in attack mode. Less well-known (or at least less well-remembered) is that an independent clause in a sentence is often set off by a comma. A clause is a phrase that has a subject and a predicate where the predicate is or has a verb ("The cat [← subject / predicate →] is happy" "My hand [← subject / predicate →] is shredded") and is part of a sentence that has multiple clauses. An independent clause is one that can exist on its own as a complete sentence. When you have two independent clauses that are linked to form one complete idea, you separate the two by a comma. And a comma indicates a short pause. ("The cat is happy, and my hand is shredded.")

CONFUSION COMES A-KNOCKIN'

Knock knock.

Who's there?

A dangling modifier.

A dangling modifier who?

That's what I'm trying to figure out!

BONUS PUNCHLINE

A dangling modifier who is selling books with grammar rules and bad jokes.

. . . .
WHAT'S SO FUNNY?
. . . .

You mean besides the phrase "dangling modifier"? OK then.

While a modifier describes something in a sentence, lending more clarity or specificity to the something in question, a dangling modifier is a word or phrase that is meant to describe (modify) something in a sentence, but is failing at its job. With danglers, it's unclear what the modifier is modifying. The first punchline pokes fun at that ambiguity, while the bonus punchline has in itself a dangling modifier. Is the grammatical salesperson selling books that contain *both* grammar

rules *and* bad jokes, or is the sales pitch for two books, one that has grammar rules and another that has bad jokes? Don't answer that.

ELF RIGHTS RIGHT NOW!

Why did Santa's workshop elves rebel?

Because they were sick of being subordinate Clauses!

. . . .
WHAT'S SO FUNNY?
. . . .

A subordinate clause contains a subject and a predicate verb, just like any other clause, but it can't stand on its own as a complete sentence because it begins with a subordinate conjunction (*because*, *after*, *since*, and so on) or a relative pronoun (*who*, *which*, *that*, etc.). While "Santa bossed around the elves" is a complete sentence, if you throw a "because" in front of it, it becomes incomplete and therefore dependent on something else to finish the thought. Maybe "The elves felt downtrodden" or "The reindeer sided with the workshop in the rebellion" could be the independent clause that completes that sentence.

It's worth pointing out that the punchline of this joke, while a subordinate clause in itself, is technically grammatically incorrect, as it is not a full sentence. But you get the full idea given the setup.

HISTORY
&
POLITICS

HINDSIGHT IS TWENTY-TWENTY, AND ON THE grand scale it can be kind of hilarious. Super serious events— war, revolution, assassinations—can have their somber bubbles burst with a little levity. Lighting things up is a great way to open the door of examination while leaving the emotional baggage at the jamb. Or for when things are really far back and no one is upset about them anymore, jokes can act as fun mnemonics to help you remember historical trivia.

And politics are always funny. So funny you could beat your head against the wall until you cry. If there was ever a topic that needs a tension-breaker you can pull out when conversations with friends, family, or strangers on the Internet go awry, this is it!

A JOKE FOR THE MASSES

How many Marxists does it take to change
a light bulb?

**None. The light bulb contains the power to make
its own revolution.**

. . . .
WHAT'S SO FUNNY?
. . . .

Communism did not become funny until the '90s, after the Cold War
ended. In the enlightened twenty-first century, we can joke about it,
and light bulbs, freely.

Marxism is the political ideology (created by the philosophers
Karl Marx and Friedrich Engels, with one of them totally getting
the shaft in the naming-the-ideology department) on which
communism is framed. More simply, Marxism is the instruction
manual for getting a communist society. Core to Marxism, and
therefore communism, is that class conflicts between the makers
(the proletariats) and the owners (the bourgeoisie) will inevitably
boil over, because the former is busting their asses for pennies while
the latter is toasting champagne glasses filled with the former's
blood, sweat, and tears (metaphorically speaking of course, well,
probably) and doing little else.

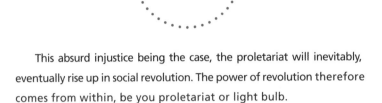

This absurd injustice being the case, the proletariat will inevitably, eventually rise up in social revolution. The power of revolution therefore comes from within, be you proletariat or light bulb.

AN <u>ARCHNEMESIS</u>?

Say what you like about the archduke, but the problems started only after we were *sans Ferdinand*.

WHAT'S SO FUNNY?

Is there anything funnier than a good assassination joke? World War I was kicked off when Archduke Franz Ferdinand of Austria and his wife were shot and killed on a trip to Sarajevo, then the capital of the Austro-Hungarian province of Bosnia and Herzegovina. While this shooting was the direct trigger (har har har) for the war, let's just say the archduke was not so epically cool that the whole world went to war over his death alone.

YOU CAN STILL KEEP THIS JOKE

Why did the anarchist Pierre–Joseph Proudhon only
ever drink horrible tea?

Because proper tea is theft.

What's So Funny?

Anarchists are usually very humorless folk when it comes to politics,
including Pierre-Joseph Proudhon, who wrote *What Is Property?* in
1840. He answered that question by saying "Property is theft!" and
probably would not appreciate this play on words at his expense. It
should be noted that by "property" Proudhon didn't mean stuff like
your clothes and your food. He meant landowners that did not work
their land and instead hired other people to work it and then profited
from their work. To him, that was stealing, because the only legitimate
source of property is labor. Basically, if you ain't working it or making it,
it ain't yours.

IF YOU'RE INTO THAT SORT OF THING

Did you hear about the guy with a
fetish for case law?

He got off on a technicality!

WHAT'S SO FUNNY?

Case laws are a set of past rulings in court cases that were established by judicial decisions and can be cited as precedent. There are about a billion of them, and the whole legal system is obviously fricken complicated, which is why you hear about obviously guilty people "getting off on a technicality," meaning for some nitpicky esoteric reason, they go free. In the case of this joke, however, it means something far more, um, corporeal. Case law is a veritable smorgasbord of technicalities, so if you're going to have a weird judicial fetish in which you "get off" in the double-entendre sense, on minute, highly specific details, this is a good one to have.

SHE'S GETTING AN A

On the first day of a course on the French Revolution, the professor asked, "Can anyone tell me a little something about Napoleon Bonaparte's origin?"

A student quickly raised her hand and said, "Course I can!"

. . . .
WHAT'S SO FUNNY?
. . . .

This famed military leader, who despite what you may have heard was of a totally average height, was from the French island of Corsica, which is located in the Mediterranean Sea, southeast of the French mainland. This makes him Corsican and the student irritatingly precocious.

THERE WERE PROBABLY SOME SWORDS INVOLVED TOO

How did the Roman Empire get cut up?

With a pair of Caesars!

. . . .
WHAT'S SO FUNNY?
. . . .

Way back in the heyday of the Roman Empire, we're talking 285 CE, Rome's conquered lands were so vast that they spanned from Britannia (now England) to Mauretania Tingitana (now Morocco) to Egypt (still Egypt) on over to the eastern side of Mesopotamia (now Iraq) up through Regnum Bospori (nowadays Georgia) and all the way west again, straight across Europe and back to Britannia. We are talking a HUGE number of provinces and client states—too huge to be ruled by just one man in just one capital. So Emperor Diocletian divided it into eastern and western empires to be ruled by himself and Maxentius. Diocletian then appointed Constantius and Galerius as junior co-emperors, which came with the title *Caesar*, so they could rule the empire in four parts.

NOT EVERYTHING WAS SIMPLER IN THE PAST

A Roman walks into a bar with some of his buddies. He holds up two fingers and says, *"Five beers, please!"*

What's So Funny?

Nowadays, holding up two fingers would be taken to mean the number 2 (or "Peace, man"). But if we're talking Romans, we're talking Roman numerals, and counting from 1 to 10 in that system goes I, II, III, IV, V, VI, VII, VIII, IX, X. So a Roman holding up two fingers is making the shape equivalent to our modern 5. Roman numerals had a long heyday, though, as they were the dominant numerical system in Europe from around the ninth century BCE up through the late Middle Ages, circa 1500.

YOU MEAN BESIDES BEST AT BEING THE WORST?

What superlative did Jefferson Davis get in his high school yearbook?

Most likely to secede!

WHAT'S SO FUNNY?

In the lead up to Southern states seceding from the Union, Jefferson Davis actually argued against secession. He felt it was a state's right to do so, and he was sickeningly pro-slavery, but he knew the North would be pissed and the South didn't have the military means to take the Northerners on. But secede the South did, and Davis became the president of the Confederacy. This joke would perhaps be more accurate if it used Christopher Memminger, who drafted South Carolina's (the first state to secede) declaration of secession, but most people would probably just raise an eyebrow of confusion and say, "Who?"

ALSO, THERE WAS NO ELECTRICITY

Why is the time in early European history known as the Dark Ages?

Because there were so many <u>knights</u>!

OK, so this is just a simple play on words really, but indeed, there were many knights questing around during the Dark Ages, which lasted from the fall of the Roman Empire in 476 to circa 1000. That's if you even believe that the Dark Ages were dark, a concept that many scholars now disavow, instead favoring the name *early Middle Ages*. While it is true that at that time there was a lot of famine and the Black Death was rampaging and the Church and monarchies seemed to prefer ignorant peasants to educated ones, the Church did keep a nice division of power going across Europe, as opposed to there being one enormous empire, and this perhaps paved the way for modern Western government and values. And while the massive peasant class couldn't read or write, the monastic class kept letters and the arts well alive, while the peasants figured out more and more advanced farming techniques (usually requiring heavier equipment and more animals).

IN FACT, THAT'S ALL YOU'LL GET

What's the biggest, best size drink you can get in North Korea?

A supreme liter!

. . . .
WHAT'S SO FUNNY?
. . . .

Since the Democratic People's Republic of Korea was founded in 1948 and its first ruler, Kim Il-sung, took office, North Korea has called its top dog "Supreme Leader." Kim Il-sung begat Supreme Leader Kim Jong-il, who begat everyone's least-favorite millennial world leader, Supreme Leader Kim Jung-un. The honorifics hardly stop at Supreme Leader, though. Wise Leader, Brilliant Leader, Sun of the Nation, Amazing Politician, and Savior are among the titles held by Kim Jong-il.

Philogelos, the Oldest Joke Book in Existence

And Boy, Are These Jokes Tired!

I mean that in the most loving way possible, as this Greek joke book is over a thousand years old and we are still using versions of jokes from it! *Philogelos* means "love of laughter" and was originally collected in the fourth century CE by two wild and crazy guys, Hierocles and Philagrius.

While the seeds of some pervasive modern jokes are in there, and the categories the authors used (wives, drunks, stupid kids, doctors, bad breath) are still popular with punsters today, there are some other gags that didn't really stand the test of time. Some were a shame to lose and some were a shame to bother writing down in the first place.

Classic Doctor Gag

A student goes to his doctor and complains that when he gets up in the morning he feels dizzy for about half an hour, so the doctor tells him to wait another half an hour before he wakes up!

(Reminds you of the joke "I went to the doctor and told him it hurts when I put my arm up, so he told me not to put my arm up," doesn't it?)

Ungodly

A guy with wicked bad breath was always raising his voice to heaven in prayer. After a while Zeus called down, "You know there are gods in the underworld, too, right?"

Just as the Prophecy Foretold, Sort Of

A guy goes to a prophet, who is not great at his job. The man asks about his family's health, and the prophet says, "They're all in great health, including your dad."

The guy says, "But my dad's been dead for years!"

So the prophet goes, "You clearly don't know who your real father is then."

SCREW THEM!

How many politicians does it take to change
a light bulb?

*Two. One to change it and a second to change it
back again next term.*

BONUS JOKES

How many politicians does it take to screw in
a light bulb?

*It only takes one politician to totally and
completely screw something.*

*You need 536: 435 House representatives and 100
senators, and 1 president to get anything done.*

What's So Funny?

American politicians make great butts for jokes, which is good because most people don't think they're great at anything else. The first punchline pokes fun at bipartisan politics, which tends to sway back and forth from Republican to Democratic rule, so legislation tends to get made and unmade as power heaves left to right and back again.

The second punchline speaks to how well and truly screwed up politics and politicians are. Nothing is ever easy, and sort of opposite to the Midas touch, many see the hands of politicians as turning whatever they touch to poop. I'm looking at you, libertarians!

The final punchline is a little lesson in just how many people hold elected federal office (and that's not counting the vice president). All of those people get involved in the creation of a law, and yet we wonder why the wheels of government turn so slowly.

I BET HE WENT OUTSIDE THE LINES

Why did Julius Caesar want some crayons?

So he could Mark Antony!

· · · · · · · · · · · · · · · · · ·
WHAT'S SO FUNNY?
· · · · · · · · · · · · · · · · · ·

The great military leader and self-declared dictator-for-life of the Roman Republic, Julius Caesar, probably, in fact, did not play with crayons (especially since crayons weren't invented until 1903). He did, though, have an affinity for Mark Antony, and one could say Caesar marked Antony for greatness and used him as a right-hand man. He did not, however, mark Antony down in his will, where he left his fortune and his title to his teenage son, Octavian. Octavian and Antony would be on-again-off-again (but mostly on) rivals through the years. If you want to find out about the thrilling and tragic conclusion, there's a play for that.

ONE HECK OF A FOOTSTOOL

Where did Empress Catherine the Great of Russia go to put up her feet during the Russo-Turkish War?

The Ottoman Empire.

. . . .
WHAT'S SO FUNNY?
. . . .

An ottoman is a footstool as well as an expired empire, and Catherine was indeed great. She was leader of the Russian Empire for longer than any other woman and oversaw an era of massive expansion gained through diplomacy and military force—the latter of which is referred to in this joke. In 1768, Russian forces invaded the Ottoman's Kabardia (nowadays Kabardino-Balkaria, a Russian republic on the northwestern border of Georgia) and, after six years of conflict, gained control over it and other nearby areas. While Catherine the Great wasn't exactly kicking her feet up on the Ottoman Empire, it could be said she was putting her foot down on it.

LEAVE MY MAMA OUT OF THIS!

Yo mama's so classless, she could be a *Marxist utopia!*

No joke compendium would be complete without making fun of someone's mama. In this case, she's got no class, which is Karl Marx's idea of a good time. Though he did not actually think a utopian society is realistic or even possible, he did think an ideal society would have no class and no states and that societal assets would be commonly owned. So, your déclassé mama would fit right in!

While this joke has gained a good bit of sustained nerd fame over the past few years as a T-shirt created by illustrators Zach Weiner and Hadley Rouse, it's been making the rounds in sociology circles for quite some time.

IT'S A STRETCH

Why did no one like hanging out with
Ho Chi Minh?

Because he was so Hanoi'ing.

WHAT'S SO FUNNY?

OK, so people actually really like Ho Chi Minh. Well, communists anyway, as he founded the Communist Party that led to the formation of the communist Democratic Republic of Vietnam (DRV), where he was president for almost twenty-five years and affectionately known as Uncle Ho by his supporters. He was so well liked in fact that the name of South Vietnam's capital, Saigon, was changed to Ho Chi Minh City after his death. So, why the joke? The capital of the DRV is Hanoi! Hence the ill-fitting gag.

THANK GOODNESS THAT'S OVER

What do you think about Civil War jokes?

I <u>General Lee</u> do not find them funny.

KEEP IT GOING

Well, what do you think about the Civil War itself?

As bad as it was, I'll <u>Grant</u> you it was necessary.
How so?

It was a <u>Lincoln</u> the chain of events that made America what it is today.

WHAT'S SO FUNNY?

It's hard to make a good joke about a war largely waged because some people didn't want to give up enslaving other people, but this one manages to pull off avoiding bad taste by making a wordplay on just the name of the general of the Confederate army, Robert E. Lee, while nodding at how unfunny the whole affair was. Same goes for the second and third jokes, which play on Union general Ulysses S. Grant's and Union president Abraham Lincoln's ("link in") names. You really can't do much with Jefferson Davis.

ROUNDLY FUNNY

What key was most music written in
during the Middle Ages?

B-flat!

. . . .
WHAT'S SO FUNNY?
. . . .

For most of the Middle Ages (which lasted from about the fifth to the fifteenth century, included the Dark Ages, is alternately known as the medieval period, and runs up through the beginning of the Enlightenment), most uneducated people thought the Earth was flat like a circular tabletop, instead of spherical like a big, watery beach ball. They mostly thought that because that's what it looks like when the highest vantage point the average person gets is a hilltop. Educated folks, however, knew the big round truth as early as the sixth century BCE and with widespread acceptance by the third century BCE. Regular folks got on board with the idea over the centuries, particularly after explorer Ferdinand Magellan's ship completed a circumnavigation of the Earth in 1522.

SAY IT LIKE A NEW YORKER

Who could General George Washington always
count on for a good joke?

Lafayette!

••••••••••••••••••
WHAT'S SO FUNNY?
••••••••••••••••••

While I can't say Marie-Joseph-Paul-Yves-Roch-Gilbert du Motier, marquis de Lafayette was actually a funny man (I can barely even say his name, though I know the end bit phonetically contains a "laugh"), he was indeed a major general in the Continental Army and a close friend of George Washington during the American Revolution. Lafayette is described as having "dignity of manner" with a "purity of character" and as being "solid rather than brilliant," so it's fairly safe to assume Washington didn't value him for his knee-slappers, but he did go to the Frenchman as a "friend and father."

A YUMMY ONE

Why didn't the Japanese trust Mussolini?

Because Benito flakes!

What's So Funny?

Benito Mussolini was an awful fascist on the wrong side of history, leading Italy when it was an Axis power alongside Germany and Japan in World War II. It's fun to cut him down to just some chopped-up fish, as bonito flakes are dried up pieces of young tuna used in Japanese cooking. Take that, fascism!

Laughter During Wartime

People joke as a way to deal with stress, and there's nothing more stressful than Nazis. During the rise of the Third Reich, people, including many Germans, were alarmed by the party's hateful positions and would make fun of the lunacy of it all.

> One day Hitler was visiting an insane asylum, and as he made his way down a row of beds, the patients saluted him. But when he got to the end of the row, the last man didn't salute. Angered, Hitler asked, "Why aren't your saluting me like the others did?"
>
> The man replied, "I'm the nurse; I'm not crazy."

War is serious business, deadly top to bottom. Even a joke could get you killed, and sometimes did. According to Rudolph Herzog's book *Heil Hitler, The Pig Is Dead*, a munitions worker named Marianne Elise K. was executed in 1944 for telling the following joke.

Adolph Hitler and Hermann Göring are standing on top of a radio tower. The war isn't going well for the Germans, and Hitler says he wants to do something to cheer up the people of Berlin. Göring glances over at him and suggests, *"Why don't you jump?"*

By this time, the war was indeed not going well for the German Nazi party—thank goodness—and people were again (if they ever even stopped) joking about Hitler to blow off a little steam. Being that the Nazis had absolutely no qualms killing people, in fact their whole regime pretty much revolved around the idea that you could solve all your problems by killing people, it is not unfathomable that someone may have been executed for telling a joke that disparaged said regime's leader.

HE'S GOT A POINT

A senator is walking down the street one dark and stormy night in Washington, D.C. Suddenly he feels the hard jab of a gun muzzle into his ribs, and a voice growls, "Gimme all your money!"

Terrified, the senator says, "You can't do this! I'm a congressman for the United States government."

The robber considers that and says, "Fine, then give me all of MY money!"

. . . .
WHAT'S SO FUNNY?
. . . .

No decent citizen finds the idea of a politician in mortal danger funny, right? Riiiiight. In a way, though, the robber in this joke is right. Government employees, the congressman included, are paid through tax money, so the very money the robber is trying to steal from the congressman was arguably his money at some point in time—if he's an honest enough robber to have paid taxes, that is.

SAD BUT TRUE

How did the historical reenactor celebrate
Columbus Day?

*He went to the wrong house and claimed
it was his own!*

. . . .
WHAT'S SO FUNNY?
. . . .

Christopher Columbus, bafflingly, is heralded to this day by many as
the discoverer of America, when in fact he landed in the Bahamas (not
America) while trying to find India (which is why Native Americans
were known as "Indians" for so long—ugh). More than that, when he
got to the Bahamas and not-at-all-America (he never set foot on America
in the "United States of" sense), there were people already there, so it
wasn't a discovery so much as it was just that Columbus was the first
European to get there. And as Europeans were wont to do at that
time of rampant colonialism, even though people were already living
there, Columbus claimed the land for Spain.

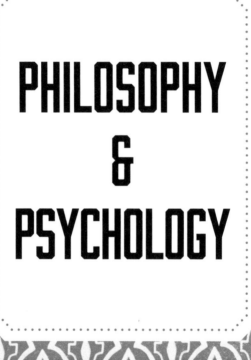

PHILOSOPHY
&
PSYCHOLOGY

THERE HAVE BEEN MANY GREAT THINKERS THROUGH the ages. This chapter takes on the thinkers who thought about thinking. Thought about it *hard*. Invented new terms to think about it. Redefined words to think about it more. Came up with charts and diagrams, platforms and schools, methodologies and symbols, systems and semantics. All of them thought really *really* hard about thinking. They took everything we thought we knew, right down to existence itself, tore it apart to nothing, and tried to build it back up with varying degrees of success. They thought so hard about things that what they ended up proving was little beyond the more you question, the more questions you come up with. Funny stuff, right!?

NERD ALERT!

Why didn't Nietzsche and Wittgenstein get along?

Because of the continental rift!

What's So Funny?

Nietzsche is one of the most famous continental philosophers. Continental philosophy being (in super-, mega-, ultra-broad strokes) the camp that includes movements such as phenomenology and existentialism, and generally thinks you can't truly understand the world and this crazy thing called life through analyzing it scientifically in discrete, little topics. Rather, all we have are our experiences, and those experiences are filtered by our own minds, which are shaped by culture, place, time, past experiences, and so on. "Objective truth" isn't really their bag. Wittgenstein, on the other hand, was in the analytic philosophy camp, which sees philosophy as a logical science concerned with language and thought and their relations to objective facts. Long story short, most philosophers would say there is a big rift between continental and analytic, and this joke nabs the geologic phrase "continental drift" to poke fun at the squabble.

A DOSE OF HIS OWN MEDICINE

Plato had been studying under Socrates for years, learning the art of asking questions to find truth. One day, he turned to his teacher and asked his own question, "Why don't you ever want to see your wife?"

Socrates turned to Plato and said, "You ask too many questions."

. . . .
WHAT'S SO FUNNY?
. . . .

Well, well, well, it turns out that Socrates, who is famous for asking all sorts of people some very uncomfortable questions, does not like being questioned about his personal life. Socrates's first wife, Xanthippe, is infamous for being bad tempered. His student Xenophon wrote she was "the hardest to get along with of all the women there are." So maybe that's why Socrates doesn't want to see her.

66 I am wiser than this human being. For probably neither of us knows anything noble and good, but he supposes he knows something when he does not know, while I, just as I do not know, do not even suppose that I do. I am likely to be a little bit wiser than he in this very thing: that whatever I do not know, I do not even suppose I know. **99**

—Socrates via Plato's *Apology*

THE LEGEND OFTEN GOES THAT WHEN THE GREAT FATHER
of philosophy, Socrates, found out that the oracle at Delphi
proclaimed that he, Socrates, was the wisest man on Earth,
Socrates said, "All I know is that I know nothing."

Humble AF, right? Well, that's not quite what he said. What
he really said is the quote above in regard to a convo he had
with a supposedly very smart guy. He had gone to that guy to
prove that the oracle was wrong and that there were smarter
men than he. Turns out the guy was full of it, and Socrates was
not impressed. Ol' Socs then went around to politicians, poets,
artisans, everyone he could think of who might be wise, and it
turned out that they were all full of it.

So, meekly, Socrates allowed that maybe, just maybe, he
might be a little wiser than other dudes (it was always dudes),
because he didn't even pretend to know what he didn't know,
while everyone else was running around talking about how
well they knew things. Then Athens got together and sentenced
Socrates to death for "corrupting the youth," but really for
being an epic pain in the ass who was always making people
feel dumb.

NEGATING EXISTENCE

Descartes walks into the same bar every night for over a month and gets totally hammered. Eventually, the bartender says to him, "Do you think you're an alcoholic?"

To which the philosopher replies, "I don't think I am," and POOF, he disappears.

WHAT'S SO FUNNY?

Descartes probably wouldn't be thrilled that his revolutionary philosophical breakthrough gets *distilled* into a bar joke, but hey it works. Descartes, in an attempt to find something, anything, that one can know for absolute certain, realizes that undeniably he is thinking, and since he thinks he therefore exists. If he didn't exist, then that thought, which is certainly happening, could not be happening. Buddhists and computer nerds might disagree, but let's not muddy these waters. Instead, let's go back to our philosopher friend in the bar, or lack thereof, who disappeared in a very Cartesian manner. When he said, "I don't think I am," he negated the very thing he said was necessary for existence. Whoops!

BONUS JOKE

I would have explained this joke before I told it, but that would be putting *Descartes before the horse.*

IT'S ALWAYS ME

What did the solipsist say when she broke up with her boyfriend?

"It's not you, it's me."

WHAT'S SO FUNNY?

Solipsism is the idea in philosophy that the only thing one can be sure actually exists is one's own mind. The outside world therefore may or may not exist in an objective reality, because one can't get out of one's own mind to find out. So, for the solipsist, everything is about them, not you.

SO YOUNG

Two young fish are swimming upriver from the ocean when an old fish swimming past from the other way greets them, "How's the water today, fellas?"

When he's out of earshot, one of the young fish goes to the other, "What the hell is water?"

. . . .
WHAT'S SO FUNNY?
. . . .

The young fish in this joke are so unworldly that they don't even know what they don't know. Having not yet thought critically about or looked closely at the world around them, they don't know about water, because water is so ubiquitous that they never even noticed it. We are all those young fish, but if we try hard enough, one day we might just grow fish ears. Bonus fact: This parable was famously used in a commencement speech by the author David Foster Wallace in 2005.

SO VERY THIRSTY

Zeno walks halfway up to a bar, but first he has to get
a quarter way to the bar, but before that he has to go
an eighth of the way to the bar, but only after he goes
a sixteenth of the way to the bar, which can happen
only after he gets a thirty-second of the way to the bar,
before which he must go a sixty-fourth of the way, **and
eventually he just drops dead from thirst.**

WHAT'S SO FUNNY?

Zeno's dichotomy paradox is just one big barrel of laughs. It's the
observation that to get anywhere, first you have to travel halfway
there, and before that a quarter of the way, and before that, well,
you read the joke, you get it. There is an infinite number of fractional
distances that must be covered before you get anywhere, and since
they are infinite, that means you'll never actually get anywhere. It's
called the *dichotomy* paradox because it's all about splitting things
into two parts.

THAT'S VOLTAIRIOUS!

Did you hear the one about the famous eighteenth-century philosopher who changed the way we think about the nature of human experience and understanding?

I Kant tell Hume you are talking about.

WHAT'S SO FUNNY?

German philosopher Immanuel Kant and Scottish philosopher David Hume are two of the giants in the field. Descartes changed the game, and then these guys took it next level. Hume, a skeptic and an empiricist, wrote his masterwork first, arguing that all we can know we know from experience, either directly or from reasoning about relations between ideas, which, you guessed it, come from experience. The skeptical part comes in when you add this up to meaning that you can't really know anything at all. Kant was heavily influenced by Hume, but mostly because he wanted to prove him wrong and get out of this skeptical impasse. He argued we know some things through experience and others through *a priori* concepts (essentially, deduction). Statements like "All bachelors are unmarried" and "All jokes are funny" are true by nature of the meaning of the words. And since our minds can perceive these truths, we can know all sorts

of things, including ethics, which was really his main bag and super complicated and you probably didn't read this far anyway, so I won't bother trying to half-assedly explain it.

JUST FIX THE DARN THING!

How many analytic philosophers do you need to fix a light bulb?

There is no answer, because that's a pseudo-problem. If a light bulb isn't giving off light, it's no longer a "light" bulb, now is it?

WHAT'S SO FUNNY?

A pseudo-problem is essentially a fake problem, a problem that doesn't really exist and therefore can't really be answered because the problem posed comes from some kind of mistake in either one's analysis or one's assumption. You can't fix a LIGHT bulb if the bulb gives off no LIGHT. A doy! This is why philosophers are so popular.

SOME REAL IRRECONCILABLE DIFFERENCES

What did the determinist and the free-will philosopher put down as the reason for their divorce?

They were incompatible!

KEEP IT GOING

What did the determinist and the free-will philosopher say when they got divorced?

Determinist: It was bound to happen!

Free-willer: This is all his fault.

WHAT'S SO FUNNY?

The ideas of free will and determinism have been at each other's throats throughout philosophical history. Free will is the notion that we are the masters of our destinies. We make choices and do what we want. Determinism, on the other hand, posits that everything that happens can only ever happen the way it happens because it is the outcome of conditions already in motion. More basically: physics. You don't make choices; the laws of physics just are and you just *feel* like you're making choices. Some philosophers have argued for compatibilism, that free will and determinism can get along, but they usually depend on warping one or both ideas into unrecognizability.

ONE SMART-ALEC WAITRESS

Jean-Paul Sartre is at a café feverishly working on his newest book, *Being and Nothingness*. The waitress comes over and asks if he'd like anything, and he says, "Yes. I'll have a coffee, please, no cream."

The waitress glances down at his work and says, "Sorry, we don't have any cream. How about no milk instead?"

WHAT'S SO FUNNY?

The astute waitress picked up on one of the core tenants of Sartre's 1943 classic: Nothingness in itself is an experience, a part of reality. The absence of something—cream, money, whatever—is the *being* of that thing not existing. This lack of something is different from something that just doesn't exist at all, such as a triangle with eight sides. Instead, it is part of a whole. You can imagine there not being a thing and there being that thing. You can imagine this joke is funny or that the funny part is absent.

IF YOU CLOSE YOUR EYES, THIS JOKE WILL GO AWAY

What did Thomas Reid say to George Berkeley?

Get real!

WHAT'S SO FUNNY?

Thomas Reid was a Scottish realist in the eighteenth century, a time when empiricists like George Berkeley, John Locke, and David Hume were running around casting doubt on, well, just about everything. As a realist, Reid believed that what you see is what you get, essentially. If something seems self-evident and is obviously the case, like I'm talking to a real person and a world exists outside my own mind, then why argue with that? Berkeley, on the other hand, maintained that all that exists, literally, is perceivers and the ideas perceived by perceivers. So cats and tables and blacklight posters all really exist— he would never deny something so obvious— they just do not exist bodily. Instead, they're all just up here (taps head).

SLIGHTLY MISSED THE POINT

Fred is mowing his lawn and he sees his new neighbor. The two say hello and get to chatting. Fred asks, "So what do you do for work?" The neighbor replies, "I'm a professor. I teach inductive logic."

"Oh yeah?" says Fred. "What's that exactly?"

"Well, let me give you an example. You have kids, right?"

"Yup, two of them."

"And you work in the city, don't you?"

"Wow, that's right, I do."

"And you're a reasonably smart guy."

Fred says, "I like to think so, but how'd you know all that?"

"Well, I see there are some small bikes propped up against the garage, so you probably have children. In the morning, I see you go down to the bus stop instead of getting in your car, so you likely work in the city instead of in town. And lastly you have multiple newspapers in your driveway, so you must like to read and people with an interest in the world and who like to read are usually fairly intelligent.

I got that all through inductive reasoning."

Later that day Fred sees a friend of his down at the bar and tells the guy he met his new neighbor, the professor of inductive logic.

"Inductive logic?" his friend asks. "What the heck is that?"

"Let me give you an example," says Fred. "Do you have a newspaper subscription?"

"No, I don't," says Fred's friend.

"Well, then, you must be an idiot!"

WHAT'S SO FUNNY?

This shaggy-dog story is adapted from a joke Norm Macdonald told on *Late Night with Conan O'Brien* way back in 1996. It revolves around inductive logic, which is a form of reasoning in which premises strongly suggest a conclusion will be true. For example, all life as we know it needs water to survive, so newly discovered life-forms probably also need water to live. Or every joke in this book thus far has been hilarious, so you can expect subsequent chapters to also be hilarious. It's not a flawless system, and when Fred gets his fumbling hands on it, it really falls apart.

"What experience and history teach is this— that peoples and governments never have learned anything from history, or acted on principles deduced from it. "

—Georg Wilhelm Friedrich Hegel

THIS IS WHERE THAT OLD MAXIM THAT IF WE DO not learn from history, we are doomed to repeat it comes from. Hegel, author of *Lectures on the Philosophy of World History* (published in 1837), learned that people, societies, governments, and cultures readily and frequently run headfirst into doom despite many, many lessons from history pointing them away from said doom. This prompted him to pen his famously biting line highlighting man's peculiar ability to make really friggen dumb decisions despite history proving time and time again that those exact kinds of decisions are really friggen dumb.

THE STRUGGLE IS REAL

Two philosophers are getting ready to go to a party, when one says, "I think this dress makes me look fat."

To which the other replies, "Huh, and here I thought we'd solved the mind–body problem."

WHAT'S SO FUNNY?

The phrase "mind–body problem" is taken a bit too literally here, but actually it's one of the few philosophical terms that somewhat means what it sounds like it means. Sort of. It's an issue that goes all the way back to the Greeks, who realized that if you think the mind and the body are two fundamentally different kinds of things (say, a soul and meat), then how do they interact? How does one control or even talk to the other? Wouldn't they have to be the same kind of thing to interact? There are a lot of answers to this problem: dualism, monism, outright rejection of the problem as a problem. Philosophically speaking, it's pretty much been dealt with. Thinking you are fat, on the other hand, remains a fairly ubiquitous problem.

ONLY A SLIGHT DIFFERENCE

What is the difference between a magician
and a behaviorist?

*While a magician pulls a rabbit out of his hat, a
behaviorist tries to pull a habit out of his rat.*

WHAT'S SO FUNNY?

At one time it was all the rage for behaviorists to try to learn
things about, well, behavior and learning by putting rats through
their paces. Mazes, food attached to electrical shockers, food not
attached to electrical shockers—they did all sorts of things to their
lab rats to try to figure out how to predict, and perhaps ultimately
control, behavior.

YOU PROBABLY THINK THIS JOKE IS ABOUT YOU

How many narcissists does it take to screw in a light bulb?

Just one to hold the light bulb in the socket while the rest of the world revolves around him.

. . . .
WHAT'S SO FUNNY?
. . . .

The DSM (*Diagnostic and Statistical Manual of Mental Disorders*) once defined a narcissist as someone who "has a grandiose sense of self-importance (e.g., exaggerates achievements and talents, expects to be recognized as superior without commensurate achievements)" and "is preoccupied with fantasies of unlimited success, power, brilliance, beauty, or ideal love." So, narcissists are pretty much the worst, but at least you need only one of them to screw in a light bulb.

THE DINNER BELL

Pavlov finishes work late one night and decides to go to the bar for a nightcap. When he gets there, the bartender rings a bell and says, "Last call!"

Pavlov palms his forehead and exclaims, "Darn it, I forgot to feed the dog."

. . . .
WHAT'S SO FUNNY?
. . . .

The Russian psychologist Ivan Pavlov is well remembered for his theory of classical conditioning, in which some normally benign stimulus, say a bell, is paired with a powerful stimulus, say yummy nom noms (go ahead, say that out loud). After this pairing happens a bunch of times—hear bell, get treats; hear bell, get treats; hear bell, get treats—the normally benign stimulus makes the subject, say a dog, react as if the powerful stimulus is happening, say salivating for the food. So, hear bell, drool.

FUNNY AH AH

Jim and Jane meet up at the playground, and Jim is looking pretty bummed. Jane asks him what's wrong.

"I just found out I have dyslexia," he replies somberly.

"Oh, I'm sorry to hear that," says Jane.

"It's alright," Jim replies, "I'm going to join DFK."

"DFK? What's that?" asks Jane.

Jim answers, "Kids Fighting Dyslexia!"

What's So Funny?

Children dealing with learning disabilities is funny, right? In this case, Jim has dyslexia, a reading disorder in which it's hard for a person to identify and decode the small units of sounds in words, making it hard for them to read even though they're normally intelligent otherwise. The common conception of dyslexia, however, is that people afflicted by it see words backward or out of order, like in the punchline of this joke, but that's really a mischaracterization.

A SLIPPERY ONE

Why doesn't Freud go ice skating?

He's afraid he'll slip!

Freud was all about the unconscious mind and the mothers, I mean *monsters,* lurking there. A Freudian slip is said to occur when someone misspeaks and reveals something about their own unconscious. Say you go to order a burger but accidentally say *boobie*, or you mean to thank your husband for a lovely dinner but somehow end up sobbing about your father. To Freud and subscribers to psychoanalysis, these aren't slip-ups in speech so much as slip-outs, as in the truth slipping out.

THE POTENTIAL FOR HILARITY

My love for you is like an action potential.

It's all or nothing.

....
WHAT'S SO FUNNY?
....

Thank you, Ms. Jeanne Turner of the Linn-Marr Community School District of Marion, Iowa, for this potentially perfect joke! Action potential is definitely an "all or none" principle. It is a function in neurons in which some stimulus, let's say a shark attack, causes neurons at rest to fire into action, electrically speaking. There is a critical threshold of voltage that needs to happen for the action potential to fire, and either it fires or it doesn't. Either your neurons get it together to punch the shark in the nose, or they don't.

A PYRAMID SCHEME

Why couldn't Maslow accept that he
had failed his class?

*Because he hadn't slept, because he had lost his
job, because his girlfriend had left him, because he
thought he wasn't as good as her ex.*

WHAT'S SO FUNNY?

Poor Abraham Maslow, he really slid right down his own hierarchy
of needs. In his most famous theory, he contended that to have
psychological health, there are needs that have to be met so that
one can feel and be awesome ("self-actualization"). You need to have
your basic needs met—food, water, sleep, shelter, pooping. Then you
need a bit of security—a job, your health, some safety net if your job
or your health fails. Next up is a bit of socializing—friends, family,
more-than-friends. The next step is feeling good about yourself—
succeeding at things and getting an attaboy every now and again.
If you have all that, then you can do things like be creative, solve
problems, and accept the facts. In this joke, because Maslow didn't
have basic needs met—no security, intimate relationships, or self-
esteem—he couldn't accept the fact that he'd failed his class. A rough
semester for Maslow!

RELIGION
&
SPIRITUALITY

THERE ARE NO SACRED COWS IN COMEDY! OR SACRED anything for that matter. All things, including things as near-and-dear as religion and spirituality, are fair game to the jokester. But jokes aren't the same things as digs. The gags in this chapter make light of the holy light a bit, but not sacrilegiously. They're all done in the good faith that they will tickle the funny bone in even the most puritanical people. They have fun with Jesus, but they don't make fun *of* Jesus. They delight in Buddhism without deflating it. They jest with the Jews without persecuting them, because God knows they've had enough of that already! Nope, you won't find one bit of otherworldly offense in here, or my name's not Frank Flannery!

A STRANGE RELIGION

What do you get when you cross an insomniac, an agnostic, and a dyslexic?

Someone who lies awake at night questioning if there is a dog.

. . . .
WHAT'S SO FUNNY?
. . . .

An agnostic is someone who does not necessarily commit to believing or not believing in God and, further, does not think you can know anything about God, 'twere God to exist in the first place. To compound this general confusion, or perhaps as the cause of it, an insomniac has trouble sleeping. And despite dyslexia not actually causing people to read words backward (see page 144), this joke plays with that popular misconception to compound the imaginary butt of this joke's problems. Add this all up, and you get one sorry chap indeed.

BONUS JOKE

How many agnostics do you need to change a light bulb?

We just can't know.

MATHEMATICS ON THE MOUNT

Jesus was practicing for a few disciples what he was going to say on the Mount. He started, "Blessed are the poor in spirit, for theirs is the kingdom of heaven. If twenty-seven minus fourteen to the power of two is equal to . . ." At which point the apostle Matthew interrupted saying, "Jesus, you know we all love them, but do you think this is a good time for *one of your parabolas*?"

WHAT'S SO FUNNY?

Jesus said a lot of smart stuff, but he probably didn't go into parabolic equations in his teachings. He was, however, fond of para*bles*, which are short stories that illustrate a moral or religious principle. There are loads of them: the good Samaritan, the lost coin, the lost sheep, the prodigal son, why you shouldn't build your house on sand, and don't hide your light under a bushel lest the bushel catch on fire . . . actually I'm not sure I have the ending of that last one quite right.

GET A PATERNITY TEST

St. Peter was doing intake at the Pearly Gates, but he really had to run an errand. He spotted Jesus walking by and asked him, "Do you mind running the gates for a few minutes while I run out?"

"Sure thing!" the ever-helpful Jesus replied. "What do I do?"

"Great!" exclaimed Peter. "When people show up, ask them about their lives. You know, what they did, who their family was, whatever, and decide if they were good enough to get into heaven."

"Got it!" said Jesus, giving Peter an enthusiastic thumbs-up.

The first person to approach the gates was an old man. Jesus greeted him and asked, "Occupation?"

"Carpenter," the old man answered. This made Jesus think of his own time down on Earth.

"Any kids?" Jesus asked.

"I once had a little boy, but I lost him."

"Tell me about your son," Jesus said.

"He was very special!" the old man replied. "He had holes in his feet and his hands."

Jesus's eyes went wide and he gasped, "Father!?"

The old man, eyes also wide, whispered, "Pinocchio!?"

WHAT'S SO FUNNY?

Nineteenth-century fairy tale meets millennia-old religion in this paternity-test joke. The old man reveals himself to be Geppetto, who was a character invented by the Italian writer Carlo Collodi in his novel *The Adventures of Pinocchio*. There have been a *lot* of interpretations of this story (just like the Bible!), but they all share a few threads that make them Pinocchio at heart. For the joke's purposes, you just need to know that in most tellings Geppetto is a woodworker who fashions a marionette of a boy who comes to life and then gets lost. By nature, the puppet would have holes in his hands and his feet for the strings that animate him.

In the New Testament Gospels, Jesus similarly seems to be lost to his mortal carpenter of a father, Joseph. Also like Pinocchio, Jesus ends up with holes in his hands and feet as a result of his crucifixion. Though losing kids and getting nailed to a cross are not ostensibly funny fodder, they are surprising and somewhat absurd links between the stories of Jesus and Pinocchio that *could* lead to the Pearly Gate confusion of this joke.

KOAN YOU BELIEVE IT?

A Buddhist monk had spent a long day foraging in the woods around his monastery. On his walk back, a farmer who was passing on an ox-drawn wagon stopped and offered him a lift, which he happily accepted. After they had been bouncing along for a while, the farmer reared back the oxen, sharply pulling them off the road and almost toppling the whole wagon.

"What's wrong?" called the monk from the back of the wagon.

"I almost ran over the Buddha!" shouted the farmer, who was significantly distressed.

"It's alright," answered the monk, "I got him with my staff!"

What's So Funny?

For those not familiar with the koan from the ninth-century Zen master Linji, this joke probably sounds crazy harsh. A koan is a paradox that can be meditated on in the practice of Zen. It is meant to cause doubt and ultimately unshackle one from the burden of reason. Koans also usually have morals, and the one this joke is based on, "If you meet the Buddha, kill him," is meant as a metaphor to highlight that studying or worshipping a deity such as the Buddha is no way to enlightenment. It doesn't mean you should actually kill the Buddha, but just your hero-worshipping image of him, so this monk's gonna have some 'splaining to do.

MISSED THE BOAT

A preacher went out fishing by himself in the ocean one day. Not knowing much about boats, he had no idea what to do when the engine caught fire and destroyed the little boat. He was treading water when a boat came by, and the woman on board asked, "Do you need some help?"

"No, my dear," said the preacher, "the Lord will save me, but thank you."

The woman shrugged and went on. A little while later another boat stopped and asked the preacher if he needed help. The preacher again said no, the Lord would rescue him. Not long after, the preacher grew tired and sank down below the water's surface.

When he arrived in heaven, he asked God, "How come you didn't rescue me?"

To which God replied, "Are you serious!? I sent you two boats!"

Part joke, part parable, this little gem pokes fun at people who are sure they understand how God works and warns against the hubris of thinking you understand His will. If the preacher hadn't had preconceptions about what God's help would look like, he would have been saved from his watery grave.

IT'S A MIRACLE!

Late one night a priest was driving down a street in Boston and swerving quite a bit. A cop pulled him over and asked him, "Have you been hitting the bottle, Father?"

"Heavens no!" replied the priest. "Nothing but water for me, officer."

"Then how do you explain the wine I smell on your breath?" asked the policewoman.

"Praise be to Jesus!" exclaimed the priest. "He's done it again!"

. . . .
What's So Funny?
. . . .

One of Jesus's most famous miracles is his transformation of water into wine at the behest of his mother, Mary, while they were at a wedding in Cana—Cana being a town in Galilee and Galilee being the area of nowadays northern Israel. The priest in this joke is claiming another miracle, this one in central Massachusetts, where there are a good number of Irish priests. And such priests have (warranted or not) a reputation as tipplers.

LIKE, TOTALLY FOR SURE

During Jesus's teenage years, Mary overheard him talking to his friend. He said, "You know I'm the son of God, right?"

His friend was like, "No way!"

And Jesus was all like, "Yahweh!"

WHAT'S SO FUNNY?

Even if Jesus had grown up in the Valley circa 1994, he probably wouldn't have gone around bragging. He just wasn't that sort of guy. But if he *did* grow up there and then, and he *was* that kind of guy, *Yahweh* would have been the perfect reply, as that's the sacred name of the god of the Israelites, as revealed to Moses. Christians argue that Jesus is in fact Yahweh, based on the New Testament's Philippians 2:9–11, which says that God gave Jesus "the name that is above every other name."

SINFULLY FUNNY

Why does it take a Catholic over an hour to
watch a ten-minute porno?

*For every minute of pleasure, he has ten
minutes of guilt.*

. . . .
WHAT'S SO FUNNY?
. . . .

While there is no commandment that says "Thou shalt not watch
porn," it's a fair bet to say such films are off-limits to good, practicing
Catholics. Catholicism is a Christian denomination infamous for the
guilt felt by its members and ex-members. It's said that this particular
form of guilt comes from the focus Catholicism has on the innate
sinfulness in people. All sinning, all the time. That's people! And not
only do Catholic teachings revolve around sinfulness, but you then
have to tell a priest all about your darkest, grossest sins if you want
to be a good Catholic. It's not an easy system. Whether it's true or not
that Catholics feel more guilt than other religious followers, that's the
popular perspective, and it's sort of easy to see why.

A DANGEROUS PLACE

Why did Eve want to move to Manhattan after
her vacation there?

She had fallen for the Big Apple!

Something tells me Eve would not have actually enjoyed New York City after living in the paradisiacal Garden of Eden, but then again, as the mother of all humankind, maybe she would fall for the Big Apple city. She did fall for the serpent's enticement when it told her that if she ate the fruit from the one tree in the Garden that God forbade her to eat from, she would gain the knowledge of good and evil. The serpent being the devil (usually portrayed as a snake), and the fruit (usually depicted as an apple in the West) being awareness of "good and evil" meaning all things, good and bad, but chiefly her and her partner Adam's own nakedness as that's the first thing they became aware of and boy did they get hung up on it.

HE SHOULD START OVER

A minister, a priest, and a rabbi ended up in the same cabin at a nature retreat for religious leaders. They decided to have a friendly competition to see who was best at welcoming new members to their religion by trying to convert a bear.

First the minister goes out into the woods. A couple hours later he comes back and says, "God be praised, I led a bear to the lake and baptized him!"

Impressed, the priest goes out next, and when he comes back, he says, "Wow, what an experience! I sat down with a bear, got him to confess all his ursine sins, he renounced the devil, and I gave him his first communion."

Somewhat incredulous, the rabbi heads out into the forest. Hours go by, and his bunkmates start to worry. Just after dark, the rabbi comes limping back into the cabin, bruised and a little bloody. The priest and the minister ask him what happened, to which the rabbi says,

"You know for boys one of the first parts of becoming a Jew is circumcision, right?"

Indoctrination into the various religions of the world takes on many forms. For Protestants, their ministers baptize them in water. For Catholics, it's also baptism, but you can't really use that in this joke because the minister got there first, so we skip to confession and first communion, which are the really big firsts. In Judaism, rabbis circumcise baby boys, meaning they snip the foreskin off the penis, which is why the rabbi had such little luck with the bear.

66 I asked God for a bike, but I know God doesn't work that way. So I stole a bike and asked for forgiveness. **99**

WOODY ALLEN, AL PACINO, AND EMO PHILIPS walk into a bar and all get credit for this quote. Who knows who really said it? Seriously, I'm asking, does anyone know? Well, whoever it was, they had a funny idea about Catholicism (I presume it's the Catholic God anyway, since that's the one who's all about confession and forgiveness). The quote has an "act now and ask permission later" sort of approach to faith and salvation, knowing that while God doesn't really make material miracles happen, if you ask forgiveness, he kind of has to give it to you. Loophole achieved!

BOYS WILL BE BOYS

With heavy heart, a Jewish man went to his rabbi and said he had raised his son in the faith, sent him to the top schools, and threw him the best bar mitzvah he could. But alas, his son converted to Christianity. "What did I do wrong?" he asked the rabbi.

"It's a funny coincidence that you came to me with this problem," said the rabbi. "I did all the same things and my son ended up converting to Christianity."

"What did you do?" asked the man.

"I went to God with my problems and asked for guidance," replied the rabbi.

"And what did God say?" the man asked.

"God said, it's a funny coincidence that you came to me with this problem . . ."

WHAT'S SO FUNNY?

God's son, too, turned to Christianity, what with being Christ and all. It could be argued that this joke positions Jesus as the son of God,

God, which the Jews tacitly don't buy. But Jesus was a Jew, and Jews consider themselves to be the children of God (Christians also consider themselves to be this, it sort of runs in the family of Old Testament–based religions), so it's within the Jewish faith that God would consider Jesus his son. They just wouldn't consider him to be the Messiah.

BROTHERLY NOT-LOVE

How long was Cain jealous of his brother?

For as long as he was <u>Abel</u>.

WHAT'S SO FUNNY?

Oh brother. The story of Cain and Abel appears in the Bible's book of Genesis as well as the Qur'an. It tells of two brothers: Cain, a farmer, and Abel, a shepherd. The two made offerings to God, and for whatever reason—who am I to question God's prerogative?—God swiped right for Abel's offering and left for Cain's (meaning he accepted Abel's but not Cain's). Cain was hella jealous and shortly thereafter took an ax, literally, to his relationship with his brother. Needless to say, God was not any happier with Cain after this fratricide.

#MEDUSATOO

Why did Medusa get called down to HR?

She kept objectifying people.

. . . .
WHAT'S SO FUNNY?
. . . .

Medusa is a monstrous lady from ancient Greek mythology. She had wings and her hair wasn't actually hair but venomous snakes, which made it really hard for her to find a good beautician, because few hairdressers were also herpetologists back then—or now even. According to the myth, if you looked at her, you would be turned to stone, hence her run-in with human resources in this joke. She was eventually beheaded by the hero Perseus, who then used her decapitated cranium as a weapon, as even in death, her gaze was a stone-cold killer.

I'LL JUST SIT IN THE DARK

How many theologians do you need to change
a light bulb?

*An infinite number because before they
ever get around to changing the light bulb, they
get caught up trying to explain how an omniscient,
omnipresent, omnipotent, omnibenevolent
god would allow for there to be any darkness
in the first place.*

. . . .
WHAT'S SO FUNNY?
. . . .

The problem of evil—which is the problem of explaining why an
all-knowing (omniscient), ever-present (omnipresent), limitlessly
powerful (omnipotent), absolutely pure good (omnibenevolent) god
allows for there to be any evil at all—has plagued theologians for
time immemorial. There are a number of answers to it—people's
response to evil determines if they're good enough for heaven, how
dare you deign to know God and his plan, what seems like evil
might not really be evil, the argument is a big fat hairy stupid butt
in the first place—but none are quite watertight and students of
monotheistic religions still wrestle with this goliath.

GO ABOUT YOUR BUSINESS

What did the Jedi master say to the Zen master?

"This isn't the void you're looking for."

This joke, courtesy of writer, philanthropist, and funny guy Skip Mendler, combines everyone's favorite spiritual leaders, Jedi masters (as in warriors from the Star Wars universe who have a good grasp on the Force, which is a metaphysical power that can be yielded to get Siths done, so to speak) and Zen masters (as in someone who has studied Zen Buddhism for a long time and teaches its principles to others). The punchline references one of the most famous lines delivered by Jedi master Obi-Wan Kenobi, in which he uses the Force to totally manipulate the mind of some stupid stormtrooper.

Zen masters have other prerogatives. Through meditation they are looking for the void, which according to the Dalai Lama, who is pretty much as close as Earth has to an Obi-Wan-type, is "the true nature of the things and events" in that all things are part of one ever-changing existence. Nothing and no one are fixed or permanent; everything is part of one single thing, and it is all always changing. According to the ancient Heart Sutra, "All phenomena in their own-being are empty,"

which roughly means that the perception of each thing or person having an independent existence is empty, void, not true, a no-go. We can spend a long time, a lifetime even, looking for true understanding of the void and still not fully cram it into our brains.

THE WRONG REASON

Why did the guru refuse Novocain when he went to get his cavity filled?

He wanted to transcend dental medication.

WHAT'S SO FUNNY?

This confused spiritual leader is probably thinking of transcendental meditation, which was developed by the guru Maharishi in the 1950s and began to spread around the world in the 1960s, especially once the Beatles started practicing it. For fifteen to twenty minutes twice a day, you repeat a mantra in your head. This allegedly gives the brain a good rest and allows it to wake up rejuvenated and chug along at full power. Celebrities such as Hugh Jackman, David Lynch, Ellen DeGeneres, and many others swear by it. How can that much money be wrong?

HOLD THE MUSTARD THOUGH

What did the Buddhist say to the hot-dog vendor?

Make me one with everything.

An important concept in Buddhism is that the self is no-self. To attain enlightenment, which is the goal of Buddhists (if they even are allowed goals and desires, which is in itself debatable and should be addressed by another joke entirely), one must understand that the division of self from the rest of the universe is false. Some Buddhists believe the idea of self is a delusion, and once you are free from that delusion and realize you are one with everything, BAM!, enlightenment. Others hold that nothing physical has a self at all, and once you realize nothing has some elemental thing that makes it *it* and that instead everything is it, then it all becomes enlightened at once. Got it? Didn't think so. If only enlightenment was as easy as ordering it up from a purveyor of processed meat!

BUDDHIST MINDS DON'T THINK ALIKE

Two Buddhist monks are meditating on a mountaintop, when one leans over to the other and asks, *"Are you not thinking what I'm not thinking?"*

WHAT'S SO FUNNY?

This punchline originally printed in *The New Yorker* in a cartoon by Pat Byrnes. It alludes to one of the aims, if not the *big* aim of Buddhist meditation, which is to totally clear the mind. To calm the mind, to transform one's thinking in order to understand the nature of things, to allow thoughts to come and go and not hold on to or try to control any of them are all part of the meditative experience. Easy, right?

RESOURCES

A lot of jokes are like folklore; they get passed around so much that it's nearly impossible to find out who specifically was the very first person to tell each one. For the jokes I could trace, I did my best to give credit where credit was due on the pages herein. For the rest, I adapted them from collections of jokes hosted by a bunch of places, including:

Business Insider
BuzzFeed
Comedy Central's joke database
Huffington Post
jokes4us.com
LaffGaff.com
LaughFactory.com
Philosophy Now
Psychology Today
Public Radio's *Prairie Home Companion*
Reader's Digest
Reddit